Praise for *Danny Brassell*

WOW... Danny Brassell! One of my heroes! Truly an inspiration and a man who is doing absolutely amazing work...Our children – and those of future generations are fortunate that he is in the world and doing the work that he is doing.

> – *Bob Burg, New York Times Best-Selling Author*
> Endless Referrals *and* The Go-Giver

I thoroughly enjoyed listening and learning (from Danny). He is so easy to listen to and so great in that he is sharing his wisdom with so many.

> – *Kevin Eastman, Assistant Coach*
> 2008 World Champion Boston Celtics

After meeting Danny it is hard not to be excited about your goals. This book is a wonderful blend of tips and stories.

> – *Terri Harden, Artist & Imagineer*
> Walt Disney Company

Danny is absolutely on fire about what he does and the people he gets a chance to reach. Applauding wildly for (Danny).

> – *Rodney Muhammad, CEO*
> Your Bakery/Shabazz Bakery

Leadership in every sector can benefit from hearing Danny, as he dynamically and with humor provides so many examples of how leaders apply their perspectives and experiences in diverse environments. His skill in linking the lessons learned by children and the ability to apply those (lessons) in leadership roles is exceptional.

– Lila Larson, Former National
Leadership Development Consultant
IBM Global Services – Canada

Impactful! From the top business leader to the essential hourly employee, Danny unveils an easy, memorable pathway to achievement.

– Elizabeth McCormick, Former U.S.
Army Blackhawk Pilot

Let Danny be your coach, and he will show you that not all readers are leaders, but all leaders are readers. He will make you laugh, cry and think – sometimes within the same sentence.

– Jaymin Patel, Consultant and Fortune 500 Advisor

From start-up entrepreneurs to the world's most powerful CEOs, Danny can and will teach anyone how to be successful and much happier doing what they love to do.

– Kevin Knight, President
Liberty Management

Danny aspires to bring the best out of an individual by using his charismatic enthusiasm, humor and motivational skills. It was evident that our employees walked away inspired and were eager for more Danny.

– Daniela Sabo, Human Resources Coordinator
AEG-Staples Center and Nokia Theater L.A. Live

I got fired up when I heard Danny tell his story. He knocked it out of the park! He's funny...has a depth of knowledge and experience...and has a huge heart.

– Ruben Gonzalez, 4-Time Winter Olympian

If you're looking for someone with high-energy to capture the attention of your audience – and really bring it home with humor – Danny is your person!

– Lavonna Roth, Founder
Ignite Your Shine

Danny is one of the most-outstanding leadership speakers, but not only that – he is one of the people I look forward to meeting with in mastermind sessions. He uses his intellect and experiences as (an inner-city) teacher to show people how to "better their best." His insight is immediately actionable!

– Dr. Tim Benson, Psychiatrist and
High-Performance Coach
Harvard University

Danny is such a great writer...because he is a great reader.

– Jeffrey Flamm, Founder and President
Infinite Mind

Danny brilliantly connects with all audiences at every level. There is no one I would rather see in front of an audience, and now he has brought the same passion and energy to this book.

– Greg O'Donnell, Founder
Business Finance & Development, LLC

Danny was the most engaging speaker I can remember seeing in all of my conference-attending experiences. He shared a ton of great, useful ideas while keeping us all smiling. The time literally flew by – how often does that happen at a workshop?

– Amy Ahrens, Sixth-Grade Language Arts Teacher
Prairie Knolls Middle School (Elgin, Illinois)

I want to thank Dr. Brassell for sharing his wit and wisdom! I truly enjoyed every second of his presentations (I attended all of them!) and can't wait to share with my teachers! I was so impressed that I went out and purchased some of his books for our professional growth library, and several of my staff members have already checked them out to read over the summer. LOVE Danny's message!

– Lisa Davis, Principal
Bayless Elementary School (Lubbock, Texas)

Thanks for such an INCREDIBLE training session, Danny. I didn't know how our volunteers (myself included) would make it through a post-workday three-hour training session, but your energy made it easy as pie!

– Anita Woerner, Vice President of
Government & Community Affairs
Paramount Pictures

Danny Brassell is an extremely dynamic speaker who is passionate about kids and literacy. If you haven't had the opportunity to hear him in person, this is the perfect book to get you excited about teaching.

– Laura Numeroff, Author
If You Give a Mouse a Cookie

I, too, suffer from a similar enthusiasm for teaching and can't wait to work with the next pile of teachers wherever I work with them. (Danny's) talk made me laugh, cry and might just have changed my life...all of the elements of a good (presentation)!

– Greg Mitchell, Educational Consultant
Major Mitchell Productions (Jolimont, Australia)

For those people who desire to move forward in life, to grow, and to expand, Danny shares the power of how reading transforms a wish into an achievement. Danny has the strength of a storyteller who entertains while weaving an educational message throughout each tale. Invite Danny to coach you from your dreams to a new reality.

– Sherry M. Winn, Two-time Olympian,
All-American, NCAA National Championship
Women's Basketball Coach

Danny's goal is to inspire others to make a difference themselves...he makes it so easy to share the details of our inspiration, bumps on the road, and successes. He is the perfect role model himself!

– Jacqueline Caster, President and Founder
Everychild Foundation

We all know that reading has the power to drastically change lives, but Danny takes reading to a whole new level (in this book). Not only is it packed full of inspirational stories, but it provides you with actionable ideas that correspond with the topics he covers. This book is the ultimate road map for leaders at any level that want to continue to grow and achieve maximum success.

– Bill Turley, Esq., Founder
TrustBasedLawyerMarketing.com

Danny's enthusiasm was contagious and his personal experiences made the presentation informative and relevant. Some people may find it daunting to energize and motivate a large group of administrators after completing statewide testing, but Danny "knocked out socks off." We were ready for any challenge after listening to his inspiring presentation.

– Robert L. Wagner, President
Maryland Association of Elementary
School Principals

Yes indeed, you need (this book)! America's Leading Reading Ambassador, Dr. Brassell shows how readers become leaders in this highly educational and entertaining guidebook.

– Michael J. Maher, Founder of The
Generosity Generation & Author
The Seven Levels of Communication:
Go from Relationships to Referrals

Thank you very much for inspiring our students to aim for the extraordinary every day! Blessings and appreciation from our students and faculty. With Dr. Brassell's help, we will create great readers into great leaders in India!

– K. Nehru, Principal
Nehru High School (Chennai, India)

Danny has the greatest collection of stories I've ever heard. He's inspiring, he's funny and audiences love him!

– Bruce Lansky, Internationally-known
Poet & Anthologist

Danny is fabulous! He will lift you, build you and move you.

– Steve Shallenberger, Founder of Synergy
Companies and Author
Becoming Your Best

Danny Brassell was fantastic! Our school in-service was the best one ever. Our morale was down in the dumps – from the administration to every school in our district. Danny made me feel important again and reminded me that we all do make a difference each and every day.

– Lori Shannon, ELL Teacher
Guymon, Oklahoma

ALSO BY DANNY BRASSELL

The Reading Breakthrough

The Reading Makeover (with Mike McQueen)

May I Have a Word?

Read, Lead & Succeed

Secrets of Successful Readers

Understanding the English Language Learner

Songs, Chants & Morning Meetings

Bringing Joy Back into the Classroom

Dare to Differentiate

75+ Reading Strategies

*A Baker's Dozen of Lessons Learned
from the Teaching Trenches*

Comprehension That Works (with Tim Rasinski)

News Flash!

Readers for Life

*Vocabulary Strategies Every Teacher
Needs to Know* (with Jim Flood)

SEMINARS BY DANNY BRASSELL

Leadership Begins with Motivation

The Speaking Breakthrough

Entrepreneurs' Writing Academy

The Reading Breakthrough

Bringing Joy Back into the Workplace

**Meet Danny online and receive free training at
<u>www.DannyBrassell.com</u>**

Leadership Begins With Motivation

LEADERSHIP
BEGINS
with
MOTIVATION

33 UNIQUE WAYS TO THINK & ACT LIKE
A SUCCESSFUL LEADER THAT WILL TRANSFORM
YOUR PROFESSIONAL & PERSONAL LIFE

DR. DANNY BRASSELL

Success Press

A division of Go Habit Pro
No 10/1. 2nd Floor, 1st St.
Chowdry Nagar, Valasaravakkam
Chennai, Tamil Nadu 800087 India
www.GoHabitPro.com

Offices and agents throughout the world

Leadership Begins with Motivation first published in Success Press 2015
This second revised edition published in 2020

Success Press titles may be purchased in bulk for educational, business, fund-raising or sales promotional use. For information, please email info@gohabitpro.com.

Library of Congress Cataloging-in-Publication Data

Brassell, Danny.
Leadership begins with motivation: 33 unique ways to think & act like a successful leader that will transform your professional & personal life / Danny Brassell.
p. cm.
ISBN: 9798649211598 (alk. paper)
1. Leadership. 2. Success-Psychological aspects. I. Title.

Printed in the United States of America
1 3 5 7 9 10 8 6 4 2

To my parents,
Dan and Cathy – my role models and heroes

CONTENTS

Introduction
(to the Second Edition)

Jim Rohn said that poor people have big TVs, while rich people have big libraries.

It's ironic that I am now considered to be a reading expert because I *hated* reading as a child.

My father was a librarian, and I always hated going to the library. In my mind, public libraries were dark places with uncomfortable furniture, questionable scents, elderly women telling me to be quiet and creepy homeless guys hanging out by the bookshelves acting like vampires.

My preferred reading material used to be the *TV Guide*.

It wasn't until I became an inner-city teacher that I realized I had led a privileged life.

Most of my students came from single-parent homes. A few had never even been to the public library (they didn't even know where it was). And all qualified for "free and reduced lunch" at my school, which was just code for "they were poor."

Shame on me.

I had grown up with all sorts of advantages that I had never considered.

First of all, I was born white, male and American. Without doing a thing, many doors were open to me that – sadly – are not open to everyone.

Second, my parents were like the ones you used to see on television. No, they were not the blubbering imbeciles you often see on today's programs. My Mom and Dad were like June and Ward Cleaver. Dad went to work each day, and Mom took care of our home. Home-cooked dinner was always at the same time.

We had tons of books, magazines and newspapers available in our home, and my siblings and I saw my parents reading in front of us and to us *constantly*. On Sundays we went to church, and on Friday nights we had "party nights," where we ate our favorite treats, turned off the TV and played board games as a family.

We were not wealthy by any means, but we certainly were not poor.

So when I began teaching my students, it soon became apparent that I was responsible for getting them interested in reading. And since I was not a big reader myself at the time, I decided that I must start reading voraciously.

Kids are not stupid. If they do not see adults reading, how do we expect them to read?

And the reason I saw so many of my students not reading – whether they were kindergartners or twelfth graders, but especially the older students – was because they were forced to read things that didn't interest them.

Don't get me wrong. I think learning to read texts about evaporation and parts of speech and branches of government are important, but none of those things are going to spark animated discussions afterwards.

"Hey, man, you gotta check out this textbook! It's got a list of all the elements that appear on the Periodical Chart!"

I don't think so.

Yes, it is important to teach people how to read for information and comprehend what they read. And I think schools, for the most part, do a decent job of teaching kids how to read. But what good is it teaching kids *how* to read if they never *want* to read?

I decided that I would be the person who showed students *why* to read so that they would do it for themselves for the rest of their lives – not because they were going to be graded on it.

To me, it is important to be constantly curious, so why do we discourage that?

Ever see a child keep on asking a parent "Why?," only to be eventually told by the exasperated parent to "stop asking questions?"

Isn't asking questions critical to our progress?

So I made it a point to read aloud stories to my students – or simply share stories I had heard over the years. These stories always sparked discussions, and these discussions served as some of the most important lessons my students and I learned over the years.

I wanted to encourage my students to be curious long after they had left my classroom. And in my haste to excite my students to read more, I ignited my own passion for reading. I read anything and everything – for all ages. But I have always been particularly drawn to stories about people who have succeeded in different walks of life.

And in my readings of successful people, I have noticed that successful people don't view reading as a chore, but as a reward in itself.

The most successful leaders – in my studies – have always been avid readers.

More importantly, though, these people took what they learned and put it into action.

It is through reading the stories of successful people and companies that I have become motivated to constantly push ahead – to get comfortable with being uncomfortable and jumping into new endeavors. In successful people's stories, I see my own.

Successful people try lots of different things. They fail repeatedly. But any setback is just a lesson as they get back up, time and again.

So, as you read this book about leadership principles and successful people, I want you to keep in mind that none of the people in these pages learned a thing...without doing something.

Whether I was teaching younger students or older students, I always implored them to remember one thing as they left my classroom: *education is valuable, but execution is priceless!*

Knowledge is not power. Only applied knowledge is power.

Knowing what the right thing to do and doing the right are two different things.

So I implore you, the reader, to not only enjoy this book. I ask that you also take what you learn and put it into action.

One of my past pastors had a better way of saying it: I don't expect you to do everything suggested in this book, but for goodness sake – do something!

Oh – and one more thing. This book grew from another book I wrote entitled *Read, Lead & Succeed*. If you're interested in that book, you can get your free e-copy at www.FreeGiftfromDanny.com. The response from that book has been so overwhelming, as I have now met thousands of people like me who yearn to hear positive, inspirational stories. So when you get your free book, give me your email address. I'll send you one positive message a week for the rest of your natural life (or mine).

Remember: the world needs to see your smile and hear your laughter.

Danny Brassell
April 27, 2020

-ation

ˌ/āSH(ə)n/

suffix

1. (forming nouns) denoting an action or an instance of it.
2. denoting a result or product of action.

CHAPTER ONE

mo·ti·va·tion
/ˌmōdəˈvāSH(ə)n/

noun
1. the reason or reasons one has for acting or behaving in a particular way.
2. the general desire or willingness of someone to do something.

> *"Strength does not come from physical capacity.*
> *It comes from an indomitable will."*
> – Mahatma Gandhi

Ever wonder what the difference is between motivation and willpower?

Motivation is a desire to take action. Willpower is taking action.

Leadership begins with motivation.

The history of progress is a timeline of dreams and goals, which are essential to success.

But any dream or goal without action is just fantasy. Anyone can desire to lose weight, but fit people make a point of exercising and eating healthier foods. Creating a "vision board" of all one wants to accomplish sounds great, but without taking the steps to make any of those visions occur is just a prayer. Even lottery winners have to buy tickets.

If there is one thing most humans understand, though, it is that willpower is hard. It's hard to finish a marathon. It's hard to maintain a good relationship with a spouse. It's hard to write a book.

But if we look around, we can see plenty of examples of people who have successfully completed marathons, sustained long marriages and written books. Numbers typically do not lie.

There are 24 hours in a day. That means each day contains 1,440 minutes. And regardless if a person is young or old, rich or poor, black or white – whatever – that person has the same number of minutes in his day as any other soul on the planet.

The difference between successful people – leaders – and unsuccessful people (label these people any way you want) is in how they use the minutes in their days.

Take television, for example. According to a 2014 Nielsen report, adults in the United States watch an average of five hours of television each day. Even a person who chooses to watch television for an hour a day over the course of a year has committed 365 hours that year – the equivalent of 45 work days – to watching television.

Can't make it to the gym? Even a person who chose to exercise for three hours a day would still have more than 85 percent of her day left. So why not take the stairs instead of the escalator? Why not embrace the last parking spot in the lot furthest away from the store as an opportunity to burn some extra calories and enjoy more fresh air? How about spending five minutes every hour at work away from the desk performing a quick set of push-ups or lunges?

A person who chooses listening to audiobooks during a one-hour daily commute to work every day in just one year's time would log the equivalent number of hours a college freshman spends in class (at least, a college freshman that chooses to attend class). People who read on the toilet for 30 minutes a day reach the equivalent of nearly 23 work days.

Productivity advice can often come across as rather drab and uninteresting when it's doled out like artificially-flavored cough medicine. And it is important to understand that what works for one person, doesn't necessarily work for another. People are motivated in different ways.

Look at successful people, though, and a closer examination reveals they do things that can be emulated by anybody.

Yes, successful people may be different races, practice different religions, live in different areas – the list of differences is exponential. However, the one thing these people have in common is their choice to establish daily routines that set them up for long-term success rather than short-term gratification. In fact, most have routines that have become so natural, they do not even view these tasks as work. They view them as part of what makes them successful.

For example, retired U.S. Army four-star General Stanley McChrystal organizes his mornings with military precision. His entire day is usually booked up with work, so he chooses to wake up at 4:00 a.m. every day to get a 90-minute workout in before he heads to the office.

Sherry Lansing, the first woman to head a major Hollywood movie studio, also sees the value in morning workouts. She says that she knows that when she exercises in the morning, she feels great and is more productive in the morning, so she tries to make it her priority.

Ed Catmull, the President of Pixar and Walt Disney Animation Studios, has a different morning routine. He says he likes to tackle the "voice in his head" before he works. He has meditated every single day for several years. Not only does it form a relaxing habit for him; it also helps Catmull to prepare for whatever the day may throw at him.

And Arianna Huffington – author and founder of *The Huffington Post* – focuses on creating a relaxing evening routine so she's wide awake and ready to go from the moment she wakes up the next day. After suffering a painful wake-up call in 2007 when she fainted from sleep deprivation and exhaustion and hit her head on her desk – breaking her cheekbone – Huffington has put her sleep as front and center in her quest for greater sustainable productivity.

Whatever your routine, you need to ask yourself if it is contributing to your success. Reading the profiles of many people from different walks of life who have sustained long-term success, I have yet to come across a leader who praised the values of partying late at night, over-eating and watching television.

Leadership and success, then, are a choice.

CHAPTER TWO

an·tic·i·pa·tion
/anˌtisəˈpāSH(ə)n/

noun
1. the action of anticipating something; expectation or prediction.

> *"He who has a why to live for can bear almost any how."*
> — Friedrich Nietzsche

A frustrated young man visited the home of one of the most successful men in town, an older gentleman who had retired comfortably after striking gold years earlier.

"I don't know what to do with my life. How do I find my purpose?" the young man asked.

"Follow me," said the older gentleman.

Silently, they trudged together to a far-away river where they found dozens of prospectors panning for gold.

"There are three types of prospectors here," the sage said. "What do you mean?" the young man inquired.

"There are those who strike gold straight away. Excited, they take their plunder, cash it in and live comfortably for the rest of their lives," he said.

"Then there are those who pan for years. They know that there is gold here and they have seen others strike it rich, so they persist until they, too, find the gold that they've been searching for," he continued.

Interrupting, the young man eagerly inquired, "What about the third type?"

Grinning, the older gentleman replied, "They are the individuals who get frustrated that they haven't found what they are looking for, so after a day, a week or a year or more, they give up, walk away and never find gold."

Slightly confused, the young man asked, "What has this got to do with finding my purpose?"

"Ah yes, the age-old question."

The older gentleman smiled and looked his companion in the eye.

"There are those in life who look for their purpose and seem to find it almost immediately. From a young age they have a clear sense of purpose and pursue their dreams with energy and enthusiasm. Some others have to look a bit harder, perhaps for many years, but if they persist and keep looking, they will find something to live for. Finally, there are those who want to know their purpose, but they become frustrated with the search and give up too soon, returning to a life of meaningless wandering."

The young man pondered the elder's words, then asked, "Can everyone find their purpose?"

"Is there gold in the river?" the wise man responded.

The young man grinned. Then, he chose his words carefully.

"So, how do I find my own purpose?"

"Keep looking," said the sage.

The young man was becoming impatient with the older gentleman.

"But what if I want to find it quicker?"

The wise old man shook his head, as he had seen many impatient young men before his current acquaintance.

"Son, there are no guarantees that you will be able to find it quickly," he said. "The only guarantee is that if you give up and stop looking for it, you'll never find it."

The young man looked despondent, feeling that he had wasted his time with the older gentleman.

Then, the older gentleman placed a reassuring hand on the young man's shoulder.

"I can sense your frustration, but let me assure you, if you can find your true calling in life, you will live with passion, make the world a better place, be richer than you could imagine and feel as though the very face of God Himself is smiling upon you," he said. "That may happen next week, next year or in the years ahead, but the search will be worth it, and your life will never be the same again. So for now, your purpose is to find your purpose."

The young man thanked his wise mentor.

"Oh, and there's one other thing that I forgot to mention," the older gentleman added. "Just as those men and women need to get down to the river with a pan to find their gold, so we need to remain active to find our purposes. We don't find it sitting around at home doing nothing."

So, now it's your turn. Do you know your purpose for life, are you still looking it, or have you given up?

CHAPTER THREE

re·al·i·za·tion
/ˌrē(ə)ləˈzāSH(ə)n/

noun
1. an act of becoming fully aware of something as a fact.
2. the fulfillment or achievement of something desired or anticipated.

> *"If you spend too much time thinking about a thing, you'll never get it done."*
>
> — Bruce Lee

The universe rewards speed.

History books are not written about "thinkers." They are written about "doers." Even civilization's greatest thinkers made sure to have their thoughts recorded.

And greatness can come from anyone, whether he is a student, a convict or an advertising executive.

Matt loved computers from a very young age.

His father probably had a lot to do with it. After all, Matt's dad was a computer scientist.

Probably because his parents would not allow him near any computers, Matt became obsessed with them. Eventually, his father relented, and Matt carefully watched his father build computers and work on them.

It wasn't long before Matt began taking the machines apart and putting them back together himself. And soon Matt started making a little money helping people fix their computers.

He made his first website around age 11 or 12. After designing a site for his jazz teacher, Matt found himself designing dozens of sites for musicians around the Houston area, his hometown.

As a freshman at the University of Houston, Matt would read blogs written by various professors. Soon, he started blogging on his own using a costly platform called "Movable Type" before switching to a free blogging software called b2 – an "open-source" program (meaning the software's original source code is made freely available and may be redistributed and modified by its users).

Besides improving his blogging and coding skills, Matt met fellow b2 enthusiast Mike Little online, and the two continued to tinker with the platform. They decided to build something that combined lots of options, was easy to use and – most importantly – was available for every kind of person.

Matt Mullenweg dropped out of college. At the age of 19 he had co-created a content management system now used by more than 60 million websites – nearly a third of the Internet.

He called the platform "WordPress."

On the morning of January 17th, 1977, Gary Gilmore – in a plain T-shirt, strapped into a chair with a bag over his head, awaited a firing squad of five law enforcement officers to execute him at the State Prison in Draper, Utah. Convicted of murdering a gas station employee and motel manager in Utah the year before, Gilmore would be the first person in the United States to be executed in nearly a decade.

Shortly before his execution, prison officials asked Gilmore if he had any last words.

Neither he nor anyone else that day would know the impact of those words.

Over ten years later in 1988, Dan Wieden – an advertising executive who co-founded the Wieden+Kennedy agency in Portland, Oregon – made something of a morbid pitch to a struggling fashion company. He recalled the inmate's final words and used a slight variation for his pitch, and seemingly everyone hated his idea for the company's new slogan.

"Just trust me on this one," Wieden implored the company's co-founder.

And the co-founder, his company and the public have not looked back since.

The co-founder's name was Phil Knight.

The struggling brand he co-founded was a shoe company called "Nike."

And advertising executive Dan Wieden slightly altered death row inmate's Gary Gilmore final words, "let's do it," into the phrase, "just do it."

The phrase has become Nike's signature slogan, helping to turn a niche brand into a global multibillion-dollar giant and etching the phrase indelibly into consumers' minds around the globe.

Leaders don't wait. They can't. They have too much to do.

CHAPTER FOUR

in·cli·na·tion

/ˌinkləˈnāSH(ə)n/

noun

1. a person's natural tendency or urge to act or feel in a particular way; a disposition or propensity.
2. a slope or slant.

> "Your problem isn't the problem; it's your attitude about the problem."
> — Ann Brashares

There once was a woman who woke up one morning, looked in the mirror, and noticed she had only three hairs on her head.

"Well," she said, "I think I'll braid my hair today."

So she did, and she had a wonderful day.

The next day she woke up, looked in the mirror and saw that she had only two hairs on her head.

"Hmmm," she said. "I think I'll part my hair down the middle today."

So she did, and she had a grand day.

The next day she woke up, looked in the mirror and noticed that she had only one hair on her head.

"Well," she said. "Today, I'm going to wear my hair in a pony tail."

So she did, and she had a fun, delightful day.

The next day she woke up, looked in the mirror and noticed that there wasn't a single hair on her head.

"Yeah!" she exclaimed. "I don't have to fix my hair today!"

· · · · · · ● · · · · · · · · · ·

In 1938, Sergeant Károly Takács of the Hungarian army was one of the finest rapid-fire pistol shooters in the world. He was a member of the World Championship Hungarian team that was expected to dominate the upcoming 1940 Olympic Games in Tokyo, Japan.

But one day on military maneuvers, a terrible accident occurred. A defective hand grenade exploded before Takács could toss it. Tragically, his right hand was blown off.

"As soon as I left the hospital, I made a decision," said Takács. "Why not try the left hand? I practiced all the time by myself, so no one knew what I was doing."

In the spring of 1939, Takács surprised his country by winning a pistol-shooting championship in Hungary.

World War II canceled the 1940 and 1944 Olympics, and it appeared that Takács would never win a gold medal. By the end of the war, Takács had risen in rank to captain. All this time he continued practicing.

When the Games were revived in London in 1948, Takács made the Hungarian team. A day before the rapid-fire pistol-shooting championship he was introduced to the 1947 world champion, Diaz Valiente of Argentina.

"Valiente was very surprised to see me," said Takács. "He thought my career was over. He asked me why I was in London. I told him, 'I'm here to learn.'"

Takács won the gold medal, breaking Valiente's world record by 10 points.

"Valiente won the silver medal," recalled Takács with a smile. "And on the victory platform he congratulated me. Then he said, 'Captain Takács, you have learned enough.'"

Four years later in Helsinki, Finland, Takács again won the gold medal. Diaz Valiente finished fourth.

This time Valiente said to Takács, "You have learned too much. Now it is time for you to retire and teach me."

There were great celebrations when Károly Takács returned to Budapest after the 1952 Olympics.

"Everybody was giving me things except the thing I wanted most," laughed Takács. "So I gave myself a present. No, I gave myself three presents. I had three right hands made especially for skiing, swimming and boxing."

Everyone deals with adversity. Successful leaders are inclined to see possibilities where others see hopelessness.

Attitude is everything. What's yours?

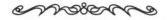

CHAPTER FIVE

in·ter·pre·ta·tion
/inˌtərprəˈtāSH(ə)n/

noun
1. the action of explaining the meaning of something.
2. an explanation or way of explaining.

> *"What people in the world think of you is really none of your business."*
> – Martha Graham

Joe Coulombe was successful.

At least, he was successful by most standards.

He started his career working for the Rexall chain of drugstores. In 1958, they asked Joe to test the launch of Pronto Markets, a store brand created to compete against 7-Eleven. After Joe ran six Pronto

Markets in the Los Angeles area, however, Rexall asked him to close down.

Instead, Joe decided to buy them out.

Always one for innovation and improvement, Joe wondered if he could create something that would better serve the growing population of recent college graduates who wanted convenience but also craved something better than two-day-old hot dogs and Mountain Dew.

So, he stocked his market in Pasadena with wine and liquor, as well as high-quality prepared foods and fresh ingredients. He hired hard-working employees and emphasized their training. He paid them well, too.

Working long, hard hours, Joe regularly analyzed his business. As the market grew, he decided to add more locations – especially around universities and young professional hubs. He added healthier and more organic foods to the markets' shelves, and diversified his offerings.

Lo and behold, in a few short years, the concept took off.

Most people know the market by the name it has today: Trader Joe's.

If there was one defining characteristic of Steve Jobs that ran like a thread throughout his entire career, it was a genuine obsession with the way that things were crafted. Not merely content to set specifications and see that they were met, Jobs frequently went above and beyond to ensure that the products he had a hand in were made in the best way possible.

In his biography of Jobs, Walter Isaacson reveals the likely source of this focus on craftsmanship: Jobs's adoptive father, Paul Jobs.

Paul Jobs was a mechanic, good with his hands and intelligent with his work – which largely focused on cars and then constructing metal parts for laser assemblies in Silicon Valley.

"I thought my dad's sense of design was pretty good," Jobs told Isaacson, "because he knew how to build anything. If we needed a cabinet, he would build it. When he built our fence, he gave me a hammer so I could work with him."

Fifty years after the fence was constructed, Jobs showed it – still standing – to Isaacson and recalled a lesson about making things of quality that he learned from his father. Touching the boards on the inside of the fence, he said that "(his father) loved doing things right. He even cared about the look of the parts you couldn't see."

Jobs said that his father refused to use poor wood for the back of cabinets or to build a fence that wasn't constructed as well on the back side as it was the front. Jobs likened it to using a piece of plywood on the back of a beautiful chest of drawers.

"For you to sleep well at night, the aesthetic, the quality, has to be carried all the way through," said Jobs.

This philosophy led Jobs to at least attempt to manufacture Apple products with the same care, even in the details that would be invisible to the user.

When the first Apple II casings were delivered, Jobs noticed a thin plastic seaming that was often the result of the injection molding process. He had Apple employees sand and polish them to be displayed at a computer expo.

Jobs even rejected the designs of the original logic boards inside of the Apple II, as the "lines were not straight enough."

Not that this stance was without fault, however. It did get Jobs into trouble at NeXT, where the precise cube shape of the NeXT casings caused huge additional production costs and heat issues because the internal boards had to be broken down and stacked, one on top of another.

"Although my Dad didn't raise a billionaire, he is a craftsman and a painter, and he instilled in me the same love of details, even those some might think inconsequential," Jobs said. "He taught me to wash the undersides of a car's rocker panels and the engine compartment, things I still do today. I fully believe that the impression my father made on me about the importance of the details has been one of the major components of whatever success I've had as a writer and photographer."

Jobs learned from his father about the attention worth paying, even to the things unseen, throughout his career and life. And while sacrifices were often made of money, time and frustration, users of Apple products often reaped the rewards.

· · · · · · · · ●●● ● ●●● · · · · · · · ·

Two leaders of industry interpreted the world differently from the rest of us.

Joe Coulombe recognized a problem and envisioned a different way of serving that niche.

Steve Jobs obsessed about the quality of his products – even down to the minute details his customers probably would never see.

How do you think differently? What's your commitment to excellence?

CHAPTER SIX

as·pi·ra·tion
/ˌaspəˈrāSH(ə)n/

noun
1. a hope or ambition of achieving something.

> *"Do what you feel in your heart to be right – for you'll be criticized anyway. You'll be 'damned if you do, and damned if you don't.'"*
> – Eleanor Roosevelt

Ambition can be a funny thing.

A management consultant, on holiday in a tiny Mexican fishing village, watched a little fishing boat dock at the quayside. Noting the quality of the fish, the consultant asked the fisherman how long it had taken to catch them.

"Not very long," answered the fisherman.

"Then, why didn't you stay out longer and catch more?" asked the consultant.

The fisherman explained that his small catch was sufficient to meet his needs and those of his family.

The consultant asked, "But what do you do with the rest of your time?"

"I sleep late, fish a little, play with my children and have an afternoon's rest under a coconut tree," replied the fisherman. "In the evenings, I go into the community hall to see my friends, have a few beers, play the drums, and sing a few songs. I have a full and happy life."

"I have an MBA from Harvard, and I can help you," the consultant ventured.

"You should start by fishing longer every day," he continued. "You can then sell the extra fish you catch. With the extra revenue, you can buy a bigger boat. With the extra money the larger boat will bring, you can buy a second one and a third one and so on until you have a large fleet. Instead of selling your fish to a middleman, you can negotiate directly with the processing plants and maybe even open your own plant. You can then leave this little village and move to a city here or maybe even in the United States, from where you can direct your huge enterprise."

"How long would that take?" asked the fisherman.

"Oh, ten, maybe twenty years," replied the consultant.

"And after that?" asked the fisherman.

"After that? That's when it gets really interesting," answered the consultant, laughing. "When your business gets really big, you can start selling shares in your company and make millions!"

"Millions? Really? And after that?" pressed the fisherman.

"After that you'll be able to retire, move out to a small village by the sea, sleep in late every day, spend time with your family, go fishing, take afternoon naps under a coconut tree and spend relaxing evenings having drinks with friends!"

Hmm. Ambition and balance are tricky things.

There's nothing wrong with thinking big. Of course, you should think big!

But keep an eye out for what truly matters to *you*. Many a leader has experienced outrageous success professionally – only to fail miserably in other areas. Define what joy means to you and guard it with your life.

CHAPTER SEVEN

vis·u·al·i·za·tion
/ˌviZH(o͞o)ələˈzāSH(ə)n /

noun
1. the representation of an object, situation, or set of information as a chart or other image.
2. the formation of a mental image of something.

> *"Visualization is daydreaming with a purpose."*
> — Bo Bennett

Did you ever notice that the world tends to be exactly how you envision it?

Want to smile? Hang out with babies.

Want to feel depressed? Watch cable news.

Yup, the world is pretty much how you decide to see it. The most successful people see success before anyone else.

John F. Kennedy had a vision for sending a man to the moon and returning him home safely – before the end of a decade when scientists and naysayers insisted the feat was impossible...

At one time, *Star Wars* was just an idea in the mind of George Lucas, but now the Force is as strong as ever...

J.K. Rowling had a vision of Harry Potter, and now he's an iconic part of our society – and as real as a roller-coaster at Universal Studios...

Ronald Reagan saw the Berlin Wall come down before it crumbled...

Sara Blakely imagined Spanx long before they became as essential clothing staple for so many...

And Maya Lin was just a senior in college when she submitted her design for a memorial to the nearly 58,000 American servicemen – listed in chronological order of their loss in the Vietnam War – to be etched in a V-shaped wall of polished black granite sunken into the ground.

You may not have such visions of grandeur, but they are grand, none the least. Perhaps you envision yourself as healthier and fitter. Maybe you imagine a home filled with laughter, where you and your family entertain one another without devices.

What is *your* vision of success?

· · · · · · · ● ● ● ● ● · · · · · · ·

Harrison used to ask his son, Russell, three simple words: "Why not you?"

The Baltimore Orioles drafted Russell straight out of high school with a guaranteed million-dollar contract, but Russell desired to some day play professional football. At a height of under six feet, though, scouts and coaches considered him to be undersized.

Harrison suggested his son go to college where he could continue to play both sports. Harrison and his wife Tammy encouraged their son to believe in himself and taught him that with discipline, preparation and hard work, he could accomplish anything.

Russell embraced his father's "why not you" mantra and dedicated himself to being the best he could be.

As a student at North Carolina State, he would begin his days at 4:30 a.m., practice for football, attend classes, show up for baseball practice in the afternoons and then study at night. Finishing his undergraduate degree in three years, he transferred to the University of Wisconsin, drove halfway across the country to get the Badgers' playbook and learned it in less than a month.

Naysayers continued to criticize his NFL Draft prospects, but Russell managed to be selected in the third round behind five other quarterbacks.

At the bottom of the quarterback depth chart on his team, Russell quickly ascended to the starting position.

And in only his second professional season, Russell Wilson led his team to its first-ever Super Bowl title.

There are countless tales of individuals who were discounted for anything from their size to the color of their skin, yet they found a way to think bigger than their temporary circumstances.

How many "little" people have tried to discourage you from thinking big? When was the last time ignorance or narrow-mindedness helped you?

Harrison Wilson's question to his son is one you should ask yourself right now. Why not you? What drives you? How big is your thinking? How can you think even bigger?

Remember, successful leaders see things others cannot. What greatness do you see?

CHAPTER EIGHT

ed·u·ca·tion
/ˌejəˈkāSH(ə)n/

noun
1. the process of receiving or giving systematic instruction, especially at a school or university.
2. an enlightening experience.

> *"An investment in knowledge pays the best interest."*
> – Benjamin Franklin

One of the most striking characteristics of highly successful people is their constant curiosity. L. Frank Baum, author of *The Wizard of Oz* stories, said, "No thief, however skillful, can rob one of knowledge, and that is why knowledge is the best and safest treasure to acquire."

Do you have an insatiable desire to learn more?

The son of an abusive father, one South African boy found his solace in books.

"From a very young age, he seemed to have a book in his hand at all times," biographer Ashley Vance writes. "It was not unusual for him to read ten hours a day.

"If it was the weekend, he could go through two books in a day.

"As (he) got older, he would take himself to the book-store when school ended at 2 p.m. and stay there until about 6 p.m., when his parents returned home from work. He plowed through fiction books and then comics and then nonfiction titles.

"At one point, (he) ran out of books to read at the school library and the neighborhood library, (so he) tried to convince the librarian to order books for (him)."

He started to read the *Encyclopaedia Britannica* and began to realize the vast amount of things out in the world to learn about. After churning through two sets of encyclopedias, the boy turned into a "fact factory," as he had a photographic memory.

His thirst for knowledge would not be quenched – nor his ambition.

Fresh out of college in 1995, he founded a dot-com company called Zip2 that he sold to Compaq, making him $22 million.

He poured that money into an online bank, and – as its largest shareholder – made a small fortune when eBay acquired the bank for $1.5 billion in 2002.

Instead of hanging around Silicon Valley and slipping into a funk, he flooded his fortune into three new companies. During a time in which clean-tech businesses went bankrupt with alarming regularity, he built two of the most successful clean-tech companies in the world.

In fact, his empire of factories, tens of thousands of workers and willingness to "push the envelope" has turned him into one of the wealthiest men in the world.

The online bank he sold was called PayPal.

He used those earnings to invest in three companies that are each now worth over a billion dollars: Solar City, Tesla and SpaceX.

And the abused boy who found comfort in books and fortune in America is a man by the name of Elon Musk.

Chapter Nine

col·lab·o·ra·tion
/kəˌlabəˈrāSH(ə)n/

noun
1. the action of working with someone to produce or create something.

> *"Alone we can do so little; together we can do so much."*
> — Helen Keller

Great leaders understand the importance of teamwork.

My friend, Jonily Zupancic, has a wonderful saying: "Who's going to hold your rope?" While just about anything in life is possible individually, it seems to be a lot more gratifying when others are along for the ride.

Have you ever heard the story of "Old Warwick?"

There once was a man who was lost while driving through the country. Trying to read a map as he drove, he accidentally steered off the road into a deep muddy ditch. Though he was not injured, his car was stuck. So the man walked to a nearby farm.

There he saw an old farmer and asked for help. The farmer replied, "Warwick can get you out of that ditch," pointing to an old mule standing in a field.

The man looked at the old run-down mule and then looked at the farmer who just stood there repeating, "Yep, old Warwick can do the job."

The man figured he had nothing to lose, so the two men and Warwick made their way back to the ditch.

The farmer hitched the mule to the car. With a snap of the reigns he shouted, "Pull, Fred! Pull, Jack! Pull, Ted! Pull, Warwick!" And the mule pulled the car from the ditch with very little effort.

The man stood by, dumbfounded. He thanked the farmer, patted the mule and asked the farmer, "Why did you call out all those other names before you called Warwick?"

The farmer grinned and said, "Old Warwick is just about blind. As long as he believes he is part of a team, he doesn't mind pulling."

To highlight its annual picnic one year, a company rented two racing shells and challenged a rival company to a boat race.

The rival company accepted.

On the day of the picnic, everyone entered into the spirit of the event. Women wore colorful summer dresses and big, floppy hats. Men wore straw skimmers and white pants. Bands played, and banners waved.

Finally, the race began. To the consternation of the host company, the rival team immediately moved to the front and was never challenged. Their team won by 11 lengths!

Embarrassed by their team's showing, the management of the host company promptly appointed a committee to place responsibility for the failure and make recommendations to improve the host team's chances in a rematch the following year.

The committee appointed several task forces to study various aspects of the race. They met for three months and issued a preliminary report. In essence, the report said that the rival crew had been unfair.

"They had eight people rowing and one coxswain steering and shouting out the beat," the report said. "We had one person rowing and eight coxswains."

The chairman of the board thanked the committee and sent it away to study the matter further and make recommendations for the rematch.

Four months later the committee came back with a recommendation: "Our guy has to row faster."

Why do it alone when you can bring others along for the ride? What are you doing to develop your team?

It is amazing what you can get people to accomplish when you get them believing in a unified goal. How can you unite your team to rally around a common vision?

CHAPTER TEN

trans·for·ma·tion
/ˌtran(t)sfərˈmāSH(ə)n/

noun
1. a thorough or dramatic change in form
    or appearance.

> *"If you want to be great and successful, choose people who are great and successful and walk side by side with them."*
> — Ralph Waldo Emerson

Nobody can inspire us like great teachers can. They seem to come along at just the right moment, at a time when we need them the most. They see potential in us that others, including ourselves, can't or won't. Above all, they give us the courage to find our own way with just enough guidance to show us that the impossible – or what we perceive as impossible – is anything but that.

Great teachers show us things about ourselves we can't see. They allow us to evolve – to change – from where we are to what we can be. Here are three examples.

Born in Liberty City (an impoverished section of Miami) on the floor of an abandoned building, Les was a struggling student from the get-go. His school labeled him as "educable mentally handicapped" and forced to repeat fifth grade.

One day in eighth grade a teacher asked Les to come up and solve a problem on the chalkboard, but Les refused and said that he couldn't.

"Of course you can," the teacher responded, encouragingly. "Young man, come up here and solve this problem for me."

"But I can't," insisted Les. "I'm educable mentally handicapped."

The rest of the class erupted in laughter. At that point, the teacher stepped out from behind his desk and looked Les straight in the eye. "Don't ever say that again," he told him firmly. "Someone else's opinion of you does not have to become your reality."

Les never forgot those words, and he spent the rest of his life overcoming incredible odds and pursuing his goals with passion and fervor.

Today, Les Brown is one of the world's foremost motivational speakers. Time and time again, thanks to that one teacher's powerful revelation, Les has lived the phrase he's famous for sharing with millions around the world: *You have greatness within you.*

Between the ages of 7 and 14 Emily developed a crippling stutter that had her struggling to even hold a simple conversation.

"I was a smart kid and had a lot to say, but I just couldn't say it," she recalled in an interview years later. "I never thought I'd be able to sit and talk to someone like I'm talking to you right now."

It was one junior high teacher in particular that helped Emily overcome her fear of speaking by encouraging her to try out for the school play. At first, she resisted the idea, but the teacher wouldn't give up on her. The teacher coaxed Emily to take acting lessons and experiment with different accents and character voices to help express herself.

In the end, those efforts paid off for Emily Blunt immensely, as she has had a successful career as an actress (even re-creating the role of "Mary Poppins") and serves as a member of the board of directors for the American Institute for Stuttering.

Bill was a typical nerdy 4th-grade introvert who always did his best to keep to himself.

Thanks to a kindly librarian named Blanche Caffiere, Bill came into his own in a way that would one day change the world forever. He credits Mrs. Caffiere for helping him escape his shell.

First, she encouraged his passion for reading by helping him explore it through the use of introspective questions, such as what he liked to read and why. Next, she'd go out of her way to source books that were progressively more interesting and challenging for him. Finally, once Bill had read those books, Mrs. Caffiere would sit down with him and ask him if he liked what he had read, as well as what he'd learned and why.

"She genuinely listened to what I had to say," he recalled.

Shortly after reaching her 100th birthday, Blanche Caffiere sadly passed away, but not before Bill Gates was able to thank her personally for the lasting impact her love and curiosity had on his life.

Whatever you are today – from someone who stutters to an introverted outcast – you need to understand that your story is not over. You are constantly writing it. Sometimes, a little encouragement can nudge you to heights you never dreamed of.

Is there anything more exciting than helping people rise to their potential?

See change as a good thing, as it has been demonstrated time and time again: a setback today, when you look at it ten years from now, may truly be the harbinger for future greatness.

CHAPTER ELEVEN

ex·hil·a·ra·tion

/igˌziləˈrāSH(ə)n/

noun
1. a feeling of excitement, happiness, or elation.

> "Fires can't be made with dead embers, nor can enthusiasm be stirred by spiritless men. Enthusiasm in our daily work lightens effort and turns even labor into pleasant tasks."
> — James Baldwin

Your enthusiasm is contagious. People want to be around you when you are alive with energy. It also makes people want to listen to you. Be the person so that when others see you they say to themselves, "Heck, if he's having so much fun, maybe I should lighten up and take things differently."

Make enthusiasm a habit, not a choice. Company doesn't love misery. Nobody wants to be around a person who is negative and unenthusiastic. We are drawn to people who are intriguing and live their lives to the fullest. If you walk around and habitually exhibit exuberance, excitement, energy and enthusiasm, people will be drawn to you. You will also be a gift to those around you, infusing their lives with happiness.

In their book *Don't Give Up...Don't Ever Give* Up, authors Justin and Robyn Spizman share a peek into why others gravitated to college basketball coach Jim Valvano. They offer an anecdote from Linda Bruno, Coach Valvano's former administrative assistant when he coached at Iona College:

> Just before the season was to start, the coach burst into the office screaming inaudibly about something, which was not completely out of character for him. On this occasion, he was waving a magazine and pointing at a particular page. He raced around the office, and it took almost a full minute for the staff to realize the reason for his outburst. For the first time in its history, Iona College basketball was ranked in the Sports Illustrated poll.
>
> While we all cried, Jim raced out of the office, down the stairs and out onto the track, which circled the baseball field, at the center of the campus. Jim held the Sports Illustrated

above his head and began doing laps around the track. As people stopped to watch, he yelled the good news – while he kept running. Soon, a large crowd gathered around the field while Jim waved his arms excitedly, running with the magazine above his head the whole time.

I looked around at the gathering crowd. Many were those that only a few months earlier thought that Jim's style might not be suited for Iona. They all began to applaud as Jim continued around the track.

Needless to say, when Coach Valvano found out about his team's accomplishment, he was overjoyed. He was excited, and he could not contain himself. But what made the coach's reaction so special was his enthusiasm. He was so over the top that he inspired a school-wide reaction, as well.

His enthusiasm was contagious, and it spread like wildfire.

· · · · · · · · · · ●●●●● · · · · · · · · · ·

Perhaps no coach in history has influenced more leaders than John Wooden. The winner of *ten* national championships as UCLA's men's basketball coach, Wooden's success philosophy goes beyond sports. At the center of Wooden's philosophy was one important rule that the legendary coach repeated often: make each day your masterpiece.

Too often we get distracted by what is outside of our control.

You can't do anything about yesterday. The door to the past has been shut and the key thrown away.

You can do nothing about tomorrow. It is yet to come.

However, tomorrow is in large part determined by what you do today. So make today a masterpiece. You have control over that.

You can be the person who exhilarates everyone around you with your unbridled enthusiasm!

You have to apply yourself each day to become a little better. By applying yourself to the task of becoming a little better each and every day over a period of time, you will become a *lot* better. Only then will you be able to approach being the best you can be.

To achieve something great, successful people make *today* matter most. As legendary basketball player Michael Jordan famously said, "Championships are won while the stands are empty."

So attack today with an enthusiasm never before seen by humankind, and make today *your* masterpiece!

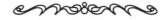

CHAPTER TWELVE

mat·u·ra·tion
/ˌmaCHəˈrāSH(ə)n/

noun
1. the action or process of maturing.
2. the emergence of personal and behavioral characteristics through growth processes.

> *"Mistakes are the portal of discovery."*
> — James Joyce

Failure is a wonderful teacher.

A wise old banker had just retired, when a local newscaster asked to interview him about his career. The banker agreed, and the young reporter led off by asking the banker to what he attributed his success.

"Making good decisions," the banker replied.

So the reporter followed-up with the question, "How do you make good decisions?"

"Experience," the banker simply stated.

Intrigued, the reporter then asked, "How do you get experience?"

The banker grinned and answered, "Making bad decisions."

When most of us fear failure, we walk away from our boldest ideas. Instead of being original, we play it safe, selling conventional products and familiar services.

But researching his book *Originals,* author Adam Grant found that successful entrepreneurs have a different response to the fear of failure. Yes, they're afraid of failing, but they're even more afraid of failing to try.

In work and in life, there are two kinds of failure: actions and inactions.

You can fail by starting a company that goes out of business or by not starting a company at all...by getting left at the altar or by never proposing marriage.

Most people predict that it's the actions they'll regret more. We cringe at the anguish of declaring bankruptcy or getting rejected by the love of our lives.

But we are dead wrong.

Research shows that when people reflect on their biggest regrets, they wish they could redo the inactions, not the actions.

"In the long run, people of every age and in every walk of life seem to regret not having done things much more than they regret things they did," psychologists Tom Gilovich and Vicky Medvec summarize, "which is why the most popular regrets include not going to college, not grasping profitable business opportunities, and not spending enough time with family and friends."

Ultimately, what we regret is not failure – but the failure to act. Knowing that is what propels successful people to new heights.

Leonardo Da Vinci wrote repeatedly in his notebook, "Tell me if anything was ever done." He might have been afraid to fail, but he was more afraid that he would fail to accomplish anything of significance. That propelled him to keep painting, inventing and designing to become the ultimate "Renaissance Man."

Successful people learn to see failure not as a sign that their ideas are doomed but as a necessary step toward success.

"I never lose," former President of South Africa Nelson Mandela said. "I either win or learn."

We learn more from failure than success. Failure is inevitable because it's impossible to predict how technologies will evolve and tastes will change.

If you're failing, consider yourself lucky. You're in good company.

In the early days of Google, Larry Page and Sergey Brin tried to sell their search engine for less than $2 million, but their potential buyer turned them down.

Publishers rejected *Harry Potter* because it was too long for a children's book.

Executives passed on the TV comedy *Seinfeld* for having incomplete plot lines and unlikeable characters.

Yes, embrace failure. It is a necessary ingredient in the recipe to success.

Looking at the biographies of some of the most successful people throughout history is like reading the lyrics to a country music song, as their paths were riddled with failures, setbacks and disappointments because they were the ones who tried the most.

Most of Thomas Edison's 1,093 patents went nowhere.

Picasso had to produce over 20,000 pieces of art to make a few masterpieces.

Oprah Winfrey was fired from her job as a reporter.

Steve Jobs flopped with the Apple Lisa and got forced out of his own company before making his triumphant return.

And with all of Sir Richard Branson's success in airlines, trains, music and mobile phones, he has also presided over the failure of Virgin cola, cars and wedding dresses.

So take it from this group of elite failures. If at first you don't succeed – you'll know you're on the right path.

CHAPTER THIRTEEN

im·i·ta·tion
/ˌiməˈtāSH(ə)n/

noun
1. the action of using someone or something as a model.
2. a thing intended to simulate or copy something else.

> *"If I have seen further it is by standing on the shoulders of giants."*
> — Sir Isaac Newton

Western cultures place an emphasis on being individualistic rather than collective. As a result, people pride themselves on being original. But when was the last time that you made something completely original?

"Nothing is original," claims independent filmmaker Jim Jarmusch. "Steal from anywhere that resonates with inspiration or fuels your imagination."

And the artist Picasso said, "Good artists copy. Great artists steal."

Copying is actually an innate human skill that we need for survival.

Heck, I have taught students of all ages, and one of the first skills kids pick up is watching others. These cues greatly influence their own behaviors. If their parents curse profusely, the kids typically emulate that behavior. On the other hand, when we model kindness and service, kids tend to follow suit.

Psychologist Albert Bandura's "social learning theory" proposes that new behaviors can be acquired by observing and imitating others. In other words, it's not a bad idea to emulate the behaviors of others. After all, businesses do this all the time.

Xerox introduced its Model 914 copy machine to the public in 1959. Back then, people used something called "carbon paper" to make copies of individual documents. Since people were used to paying for sheets of carbon paper, they were reluctant to buy an expensive copy machine and pay upfront.

So Xerox decided to lease the equipment at a relatively low cost and charge a per-copy fee instead.

In other words, because they were unsuccessful in introducing a new business model where customers paid for the machine and its parts, they decided to copy the pricing structure of carbon paper.

Similarly, when Gillette first started selling razor blades, consumers thought the product was too expensive. At that time, paying on a per-shave basis in barbershops was the norm.

So Gillette revised their model to sell the razors cheaply and profit from the blades instead, making the consumers pay for the shave instead of the device.

Sound familiar? That same pricing model is used today for selling coffee machines, water filters and computer printers where the hardware is sold at a relatively cheap price, while profits are made from selling the cartridges.

And then there are the companies and entrepreneurs that model their offerings based largely on their competition.

Take Sega.

Back in the 1990s, Nintendo was the undisputed king of home video games, accounting for nearly 90 percent of America's $3 billion video game industry. In his book *Console Wars: Sega, Nintendo, and the Battle That Defined a Generation*, author Blake J.

Harris examines how Sega created the game *Sonic the Hedgehog* to compete against Nintendo's popular *Super Mario*. By 2016, while Nintendo showed annual revenue of $4.5 billion, Sega had significantly cut into Nintendo's market share, generating revenue of $3.12 billion.

In 1994 Pizza Hut accepted the first-ever online pizza order with its digital ordering hub, "PizzaNet." By 2007, one of Pizza Hut's competitors – Papa John's – garnered nearly $400 million in annual sales.

And while the Jonas Brothers and One Direction may be among today's most popular "boy bands," they did not originate the concept. From Boyz II Men to the Jackson 5, the Monkees to the Beatles, boy bands are nothing new. In fact, the earliest forerunner of boy-band music began in the late 19th century as a cappella barbershop quartets.

To succeed, you do not necessarily have to have an original idea. You can copy someone else's, instead.

CHAPTER FOURTEEN

ob·ser·va·tion
/ˌäbzərˈvāSH(ə)n/

noun
1. the action or process of observing something or someone carefully or in order to gain information.
2. a remark, statement, or comment based on something one has seen, heard, or noticed.

> *"You can observe a lot by just watching."*
> — Yogi Berra

Successful leaders understand that the world is what you make of it, and they pay careful attention to the world around them.

Some undergraduates were attending their first university biochemistry class.

They all gathered around the lab table with a urine sample. Professor Thompson dipped his finger in urine and tasted it in his own mouth. Then he asked the students to do the same.

The students hesitated for several minutes, but at last every one dipped a finger in the urine sample and tasted it.

When everyone finished, the professor looked at them.

"The most important quality in science is observation," he said. "I dipped my middle finger in the urine but tasted the index finger. Today you just learned the power of paying attention."

· · · · · · · · · · ● · · · · · · · · · · ·

In 1907 there was a great need in America for private messenger and delivery services. To help meet this need, an enterprising 19-year-old named James E. ("Jim") Casey borrowed $100 and established the American Messenger Company in Seattle, Washington.

In response to telephone calls received at his basement headquarters, Jim and his cadre of teenage "messengers" ran errands, delivered packages and carried notes, baggage and trays of food from restaurants. They made most deliveries on foot and used bicycles for longer trips.

In 1913 the company acquired its first delivery car, a Model T Ford, and on its side was inscribed a new name, "Merchants Parcel Delivery," as a result of Jim Casey's agreement to merge with competitor Evert ("Mac") McCabe and shift the focus of the business from messages to packages.

The business began to grow quickly, and by 1919 it made its first expansion beyond Seattle to Oakland, California. There it adopted the name it still has today, "United Parcel Service," or UPS – for short.

Jim Casey's hundred-dollar investment spurned a company that is valued today at nearly $80 billion, with annual revenue of over $50 billion. Not bad, huh?

⋯⋯⋯●⋯⋯⋯

One beautiful Spring day, a young man arrived in town and happened upon an elderly lady in the town square. The woman smiled at the stranger, put aside her knitting and invited the young man to rest his feet and sit down.

"Excuse me, ma'am, but I'm considering moving here," said the stranger. "Would you mind telling me what the people are like around here?"

"What are the people like where you've come from?" replied the kindly octogenarian, answering the young man's question with another question.

"They're a terrible lot," he said. "Troublemakers all, and lazy, too…the most selfish people in the world! And not a one of them to be trusted. I'm happy to be leaving behind that horrible place!"

"Is that so?" the elderly lady responded. "Well, I'm afraid that you'll find the same sort of folks in this town, as well."

Disappointed, the young man thanked the woman for her candidness, stood up and trudged on his way, as the elderly woman nodded and returned to her knitting.

A couple of hours later, another young man, coming from the same direction, greeted the elderly woman. Again, the woman smiled at the stranger, put aside her knitting and invited the young man to rest his feet and sit down.

"Excuse me, ma'am, but I'm considering moving here," said the stranger. "Would you mind telling me what the people are like around here?"

"What are the people like where you've come from?" answered the woman, once again.

"Oh, they are the best people in the world," replied the animated young man. "Hard-working, honest and friendly. I'm sorry to be leaving them."

"Don't you worry for a second," said the wise lady. "You'll find the same sort of people here, too."

Successful people are observant. They pay attention to the opportunities around them. Indeed, they have the ability to always see the possibilities that other less observant people fail to recognize.

How do you see the world around you? Maybe even more importantly, are you surrounding yourself with others that will make your life damp and dreary or bright and sunny?

CHAPTER FIFTEEN

sim·pli·fi·ca·tion
/ˌsimpləfəˈkāSH(ə)n/

noun
1. the process of making something simpler or easier to do or understand.

> "The height of sophistication is simplicity."
> — Clare Boothe Luce

We may live in complex times, but history shows us that some of the greatest solutions to difficult problems lie in their simplicity.

Legend has it that Alexander the Great marched his army into Gordium, the Phrygian capital of modern-day Turkey, in 333 B.C. Upon his arrival, he encountered a wagon that had once belonged to Gordius – the father of the celebrated King Midas.

The wagon's yoke had been tied with elaborate knots.

An oracle had declared that the person who could untie "the Gordian knot" would become ruler over all of Asia.

Many before had tried to unravel the knot and failed, but Alexander was not one to be denied.

After wrestling with the knots unsuccessfully for a time, he announced: "It makes no difference how they are loosed."

Then, he took out his sword and sliced the Gordian knot in half.

No one had ever thought of that before.

Alexander went on to conquer most of Asia before his death at age 32.

· · · · · · · · · ● ● ● · · · · · · · · · ·

In 2012, the residents of the International Space Station had a problem.

One of the station's four gigantic solar-paneled gen-erators had broken down.

Armed with the finest and most expensive technol-ogy available, the astronauts headed outside their floating home to replace the disabled power generator. Unfortunately, some metal shavings had accumulated around the bolts of the aging unit, and none of their state-of-the-art hardware could remove them.

The situation was dire. Without a way to remove the shavings, the crew faced an impending shutdown of all of their systems.

"If only there was a tiny, hand-held brush somewhere on board!" one astronaut raged.

Another astronaut looked at his crewmate quizzically.

"You mean – like a toothbrush?" he inquired.

"No, fool!" his colleague barked. "Something light-weight – with small bristles – that one of us could easily carry out here into the silent infinity of space to clear out these cursed metal shavings!"

"So," the other astronaut stated, flatly. "A toothbrush."

Everyone on the International Space Station grew silent, as they pondered the simple solution.

Eventually, using a toothbrush taped to a metal grip, the astronauts cleared away the metal shavings, replaced the broken unit and restored full power to the station – averting certain disaster.

Of course, no one revealed whose toothbrush they used.

············●●●●●●●●●●●············

Inspiration can come in many different forms. Sometimes, the message can be very direct, as was the case with Jay Sorensen.

In 1989, Sorensen was pulling out of a coffee shop drive-through on the way to his daughter's school, and a coffee spill burned his fingers – forcing him to release a scalding cup of coffee onto his lap.

At the time, he was struggling as a realtor in the years since closing his family-owned service station in Portland, Oregon. While the coffee accident was unfortunate, it gave him the germ of an innovative idea: there had to be a better way to drink coffee on the go.

Sorensen initially set out to design an insulated cup that could replace paper cups and Styrofoam cups, which were slowly being phased out as cities across the United States began to ban polystyrene food containers. But he couldn't figure out an efficient way to package the cups for clients.

He also reasoned that not all coffee drinks needed that much insulation, as items like iced coffee drinks and lattes weren't hot enough. The cup idea wouldn't be economical for stores; it would have to go.

So Sorensen went back to the drawing board and decided instead to design a simple sleeve of cardboard to fit around a standard coffee cup. He gave his invention a catchy name, the "Java Jacket."

Sorensen made his first sale out of the trunk of his car to the Oregon chain Coffee People. A few weeks later, he and his wife Colleen went to a coffee trade show in Seattle and sold 100 cases in just 30 minutes.

Success accelerated from there. In the first year alone, he enlisted more than 500 clients who were eager to protect the hands of their coffee-driven customers.

Today, approximately 1 billion Java Jackets are sold each year to more than 1,500 clients.

The insulating sleeve of the Java Jacket is made from waffle-textured recycled cardboard, a very easy recipe to follow. While the problem was common, the solution was simple.

There's a concept all leaders should heed known as "Occam's razor." Developed by the 14th century English Franciscan friar William of Ockham, it boils down to this:

The simplest solution is most likely the right one.

What simple solutions are you ignoring?

CHAPTER SIXTEEN

el·e·va·tion
/ˌeləˈvāSH(ə)n/

noun
1. the action or fact of elevating or being elevated.
2. the degree to which something is raised.

> *"Quality is not an act; it is a habit."*
> — Aristotle

When the Ritz-Carlton Hotels won the Malcolm Baldrige National Quality Award, the owner of that outstanding organization, William Johnson, stated that now they would need to work even harder to earn the respect that came with the award.

"Quality," he said, "is a race with no finish line."

He is correct. Competitive excellence requires 100% all of the time.

Ever tracked the consequences of "almost, but not quite?"

According to researcher Natalie Gabal, if 99.9% were considered good enough, then this year alone:

- 2,000,000 documents would be lost by the IRS;
- 12 babies would be given to the wrong parents each day;
- 291 pacemaker operations would be performed incorrectly;
- 20,000 incorrect drug prescriptions would be written.

That's just a few examples.

So, with that knowledge, ask yourself, "Is it ever alright to give anything less than my best effort?"

You're too great to settle. Expect the best, and give your best.

Anything less would be catastrophic.

············●●●●●●●●······

Philippe was born with a silver spoon in his mouth.

The second son of a French duke, he grew up in castles and manors as the son of Pozzo di Borgo and the Marquis de Vogüé. He attended the best schools in France, worked as a manager at the famed French winery Moët and Chandon and eventually became director for the Champagne Pommery.

But in 1993, it all came crashing down.

At the age of 42, Philippe broke his spine in a paragliding accident in the Swiss Alps.

His injuries left him a quadriplegic. Between that and his wife's death of cancer shortly afterwards, the millionaire sank into depression.

That's when he hired Abdel Sellou, an Algerian immigrant, as his caretaker. In his early 20s, Abdel was an ex-con man who had recently been released from prison.

When they met, Philippe saw Abdel as "intolerable, vain and arrogant," but he saw something else in him.

"He didn't feel sorry for me – he was irreverent, cheeky and had an outrageous sense of humor," Philippe said.

Abdel's honest, unfiltered approach was exactly what Philippe wanted. The odd couple became unlikely close friends.

"We were two desperadoes looking for a way out: the wealthy quadriplegic and a young guy straight from jail who wanted to wreck everything," Philippe said. "Two guys on the margin of society who came to depend on one another."

After ten years together, both found their soulmates and moved on from their business relationship but still remained friends. Both wrote memoirs that have become movies in France, Argentina and even India. Actors Bryan Cranston and Kevin Hart starred in the hit American version, known as *The Upside.*

"According to (Abdel's memoirs) I have changed his life," wrote Philippe. "That may be true, but in any case, what I am certain of is that he changed mine."

He learned that real disability does not lie in a wheelchair, but in loneliness.

For Abdel, Philippe is his wheelchair Buddha: "When you help others, others help you. Only when I learned respect did people begin to respect me."

So what are you waiting for? Find someone to lift up. Like I always used to tell my students: the best way to make a friend is to be a friend.

CHAPTER SEVENTEEN

ded·i·ca·tion
/ˌdedəˈkāSH(ə)n/

noun
1. the quality of being dedicated or com-
    mitted to a task or purpose.

> *"You may not control all the events that happen to
> you, but you can decide not to be reduced by them."*
> — Maya Angelou

It had never happened before.

Never before in NCAA tournament history had a No.
1 seed ever lost to a No. 16 seed.

The University of Virginia (UVA) men's basketball
team's loss to the University of Maryland-Baltimore
County (UMBC) was humiliating and embarrassing,
and fans and critics called for Virginia coach Tony

Bennett to resign. Even though his best player could not play due to injury, Bennett took full responsibility for the loss. He made no excuses and blamed no one for the calamity.

At that agonizing press conference, Coach Bennett planted seeds for his team to heed.

"Weeping may endure for the night," he quoted Psalm 30:5 from the Bible. "But joy comes in the morning."

The setback made the team bond in a special way and made Bennett closer to his family – and his faith.

During the off-season, he got to work. He and his coaching staff installed a new offense that capitalized on the diverse abilities of its players. The new offensive sets allowed for more freedom for his players and resulted in UVA's offensive efficiency jumping from 30th to second in the nation.

Bennett and his team chose not to ignore their loss to UMBC. Rather, they framed it as a temporary setback on their path to glory. They understood that the things worth having in life are the things that require the most work, endurance and patience.

And the following year, out of the ashes of enduring the most humiliating loss in the history of the NCAA tournament, they overcame that devastating setback to win their school's first NCAA men's college basketball championship.

That had never happened before, either.

········●·········

One day a farmer's donkey fell down into a well.

The animal cried piteously for hours as the farmer tried to figure out what to do. Finally, he decided the animal was old and the well needed to be covered up anyway; it just wasn't worth it to retrieve the donkey.

The farmer invited all his neighbors to come over and help him. They all grabbed a shovel and began to shovel dirt into the well. At first, the donkey realized what was happening and cried horribly. Then, to everyone's amazement, he quieted down.

A few shovel loads later, the farmer finally looked down the well and was astonished at what he saw.

With every shovel of dirt that fell on his back, the donkey was doing something amazing. He would shake it off and take a step up. As the farmer's neighbors continued to shovel dirt on top of the animal, the donkey continued to shake it off and take a step up.

Pretty soon, everyone was flabbergasted as the donkey stepped up over the edge of the well and trotted off!

So remember this: life is going to shovel dirt on you – all kinds of dirt. Maybe you suffered a humiliating defeat in the NCAA men's basketball tournament, or perhaps you messed-up an important presentation at work.

The trick successful leaders understand is to not get bogged down by it. We can get out of the deepest wells by not stopping and by never giving up.

So if you feel like plenty of dirt has been thrown on you, I urge you to shake it off – and take a step up!

CHAPTER EIGHTEEN

dif·fer·en·ti·a·tion

/ˌdifəˌren(t)SHēˈāSH(ə)n/

noun
1. the action or process of differentiating.
2. the state of being distinct.

> *"In order to be irreplaceable, one must always be different."*
> — Coco Chanel

You're unique.

In Homer's epic poem *The Odyssey*, the sirens were mythical, evil creatures (half-bird and half-women), who lived on an island surrounded by submerged, jagged rocks. As ships approached the island, the sirens would sing beautiful seductive songs, luring the sailors to their deaths.

When Odysseus' ship approached the island, he ordered his crew to fill their ears with wax to escape the lure of the sirens' songs. This done, he commanded them to bind him to the mast as they passed the island so that he could not change his orders.

On another occasion, however, when the ship of Orpheus sailed by that same island, Orpheus sang a song of his own that was so beautiful and divine that his sailors did not even listen to the sirens' music!

You are beautiful in your own way, and the world needs you to share your gift. Whether it's the song you sing or the laughter you bring, the kindness you show or the gardens you grow – make sure to share your gift – your uniqueness…today, and every day.

· · · · · · · · ⬤ · · · · · · · ·

A lot of people thought it was the hair.

True, the hair made him difficult to miss. To say he was "eccentric" would be a gross understatement. Between the hair and tattoos and body piercings and an array of other antics, he stood out from the crowd.

But what really made him stand out – what those who worked with him admired most, was one number that differentiated him from everybody else in his era: 11,954.

By his third year at his job, he recognized his proficiency in one specific skillset of his profession that he worked tirelessly to perfect. He challenged himself to learn the specific tendencies of his colleagues.

In his esteemed career he led his company to the pinnacle five times while taking top individual honors in his specialty seven times. To this day he is still considered one of the greatest at his forte.

But casual observers will probably never remember him for that.

They'll remember the crazy-colored hair. They'll remember his affairs with celebrities and other escapades away from the office.

True, he'll probably best be remembered for his zaniness. But none of that would have happened without his dedication to his craft.

He would often head to the gym late at night with friends and encourage them to shoot the basketball from different places on the court so he could track the trajectories of their different shots. He studied film of individual players' forms from across the league so he understood their tendencies. And he learned how to put himself in the perfect position to get the ball.

He had a gift for rebounding the basketball. In 159 games he recorded 20+ rebounds – more than any other player in the modern era of the NBA. All told, he grabbed 11,954 rebounds in a career that earned him seven rebounding titles – his last at the age of 36 – and a spot in the Naismith Memorial Basketball Hall of Fame.

As a member of the Detroit Pistons, he won two NBA titles. That's where he established his defensive prowess and knack for rebounding.

But it was his time helping Michael Jordan, Scottie Pippen and his other Chicago Bulls teammates win three consecutive championships, that probably most distinguished the career of the rebounding savant known as Dennis Rodman.

··········●···········

Located in the Eastern Himalayas between Tibet and India, the tiny country of Bhutan has fewer citizens than Charlotte, North Carolina. Its economy is largely based on agriculture, but since it lacks access to the sea – and its landscape varies from hilly to ruggedly mountainous, Bhutan has not been able to benefit from significant trading of its produce.

In Bhutan, many people live in poverty, and youth unemployment is high. Its total Gross Domestic Product is $2 billion – half that of Springfield, Ohio.

By many others' measures, Bhutan is a "poor country."

So they decided to do something about that.

In 1972, the 4th King of Bhutan – King Jigme Singye Wangchuck – declared, "Gross National Happiness (GNH) is more important than Gross Domestic Product (GDP)."

The young Buddhist king understood that his tiny nation could never distinguish itself as an economic world leader. So he opted to focus on what made his country – his people – unique. The concept of GNH implies that sustainable development should take a holistic approach towards notions of progress and give equal importance to non-economic aspects of wellbeing. Its nine domains include: (1) psychological wellbeing, (2) health, (3) education, (4) time use, (5) cultural diversity and resilience, (6) good governance, (7) community vitality, (8) ecological diversity and resilience and (9) living standards.

The GNH concept has inspired a modern political happiness movement worldwide. Through the contributions of several Western and Eastern scholars, economists and politicians, the concept has evolved into a socioeconomic development model.

You are unique. You are different. Why focus on what you are incapable of doing? You're meant for so much more than that. Successful leaders utilize their unique strengths.

Embrace what makes you different, and share it with the world.

CHAPTER NINETEEN

com·mu·ni·ca·tion

/kəˌmyo͞onəˈkāSH(ə)n/

noun
1. the imparting or exchanging of information or news.

> "Anything that's human is mentionable, and anything that is mentionable can be more manageable. When we can talk about our feelings, they become less overwhelming, less upsetting, and less scary. The people we trust with that important talk can help us know that we are not alone."
> — Fred Rogers

The older I get, the more I realize that the most important way to inspire anyone is through building relationships. The old adage "People won't care what you know until they know that you care" seems to prove true.

Communication is the key, and unsuccessful people are locked out.

Teaching young children has always humbled me.

The silliest thing I ever asked my first graders to do was to write a story about their lives one day. They looked at me like I was from outer space.

"We're only six," one little boy said. "Nothing has happened to us."

"Not true," I replied. "When I was in first grade, I had this teacher who yelled at me one day, smacked me on my hand and called me 'stupid' in front of my classmates."

My students looked at me in shock, as I continued.

"So the next day I was walking to school with an apple, and I peed on the apple and gave it to my teacher when I got to school. Later that day she told me she had eaten the apple, and it was one of the best apples she had ever had."

My students looked at me collectively with huge grins on their faces, and even one boy slowly uttered, "That…is….awesome!"

I realized that If I wanted my students to open up about their lives, I had to open up about my own.

From that day on, I learned that the best way to really teach anything was to share personal stories with my students. In that way, we connected.

I also never accepted food from any of my students.

・・・・・・・・・●・・・・・・・・・・・

Like the Tango dance, it takes two to communicate. Successful leaders understand that just because they say something doesn't necessarily mean it has been understood.

Indeed, after delivering over 3,000 speeches around the world, it has become clear to me that what I say and what others hear are not always the same thing. Quite often, communication degenerates into a bad game of "Grapevine," where the final message has little to do with what was originally said.

Experienced leaders realize that it pays to ask questions to make certain that people comprehend what they are saying.

The famous movie director Cecil B. DeMille would certainly agree.

DeMille, the director of such 1950s Hollywood blockbusters as the Academy Award-winning films *The Greatest Show on Earth* and *Sunset Boulevard*, was filming his latest epic feature, *The Ten Commandments*. He positioned six cameras at various points to pick up the overall action, plus an additional five cameras to film plot developments involving the major characters.

The enormous cast had begun rehearsing their scene at 6 a.m. They went through it four times, and now it was late afternoon. The sun was setting, and there was just enough light to capture the shot.

DeMille looked over the panorama, saw that all was right and shouted, "Action!"

One hundred extras charged up the hill. Another hundred extras came storming down the same hill to do mock battle.

In another location, Roman centurions lashed and shouted at two hundred slaves who labored to move a huge stone monument toward its resting place.

Meanwhile, the principal characters acted out, in close-up, their reactions to the battle on the hill. Their words were drowned out by the noise around them, but the dialogue was to be dubbed-in later.

It took fifteen minutes to complete the incredible scene. When it was over, DeMille yelled, "Cut!"

He turned to his assistant with a huge grin from ear to ear.

"That was great!" he said.

"It was, C.B.," the assistant yelled back. "It was fantastic! Everything went off perfectly!"

The delighted DeMille turned to face the head of his camera crew to find out if all the cameras had picked up what they had been assigned to film. He waved to the camera crew supervisor.

From the top of the hill, the camera supervisor waved back, raised his megaphone and called out, "Ready when you are, C.B!"

· · · · · · ·●●●·●●●· · · · · · · ·

But you don't have to direct an epic movie to understand the value of good communication. Ask any married couple.

A man and his wife had been arguing all night, and – as bedtime approached – neither was speaking to the other. It was not unusual for the pair to continue this war of silence for two or three days!

However, on this occasion the man was concerned; he needed to be awake at 4:30 the next morning to catch an important flight. Being a very heavy sleeper, he normally relied on his wife to wake him.

Cleverly – so he thought – while his wife was in the bathroom, he wrote on a piece of paper: "Please wake me at 4:30 a.m. – I have an important flight to catch."

He put the note on his wife's pillow, then turned over and went to sleep.

The man awoke the next morning and looked at the clock. It was 8:00 a.m.! Enraged that he had missed his flight, he was about to go in search of his errant wife to give her a piece of his mind, when he spotted a handwritten note on his bedside cabinet.

The note said: "It's 4:30 a.m. – get up."

Whether it's teaching a bunch of six-year-old kids, directing for the silver screen or speaking with a spouse, effective communication is the basis for any successful venture.

CHAPTER TWENTY

af·firm·a·tion

/ˌafərˈmāSH(ə)n/

noun
1. the action or process of affirming something or being affirmed.
2. emotional support or encouragement.

> *"It's the repetition of affirmations that leads to belief. And once that belief becomes a deep conviction, things begin to happen."*
> – Claude M. Bristol

A gentleman was walking through an elephant camp, and he spotted that the elephants weren't being kept in cages or held by the use of chains. All that was holding them back from escaping the camp was a small piece of rope tied to one of their legs.

As the man gazed upon the elephants, he was completely confused as to why the elephants didn't just use their strength to break the rope and escape the camp. They could easily have done so, but instead, they didn't try to at all.

Curious and wanting to know the answer, he asked a trainer nearby why the elephants were just standing there and never tried to escape.

"When they're very young and much smaller we use the same size rope to tie them and, at that age, it's enough to hold them," the trainer replied. "As they grow up, they're conditioned to believe they can't break away. They believe the rope can still hold them, so they never try to break free."

The only reason that the elephants weren't breaking free and escaping from the camp was that over time they adopted the belief that it just wasn't possible.

Beliefs are a powerful thing. No matter how much the world tries to hold you back, always continue with the belief that what you want to achieve is possible. Believing you can become successful is the most important step in actually achieving it.

You've got this.

Partner and co-writer with Frederick Loewe, Alan Jay Lerner was responsible for some of Broadway's greatest hit musicals, including *My Fair Lady*, *Gigi* and *Camelot*.

In his autobiography *The Street Where I Live*, he explained his inspiration for the painfully poignant lyrics of the *Camelot* song "How to Handle a Woman," sung by King Arthur at a point when he is tragically both lost and losing his wife Guinevere to his best friend, Sir Lancelot.

"By the middle of the first act, Guinevere has met Lancelot and has begun behaving in a manner that is to Arthur both perplexing and maddening. Alone on stage, he musically soliloquizes his confusion and out of desperation resolves it for himself in an uncomplicated reaffirmation of love in a song called 'How to Handle a Woman,'" Lerner writes. "I had had that idea for two or three years, but I cannot claim sole inspiration for it. My silent partner was Erich Maria Remarque (author of *All Quiet on the Western Front*)."

Remarque had just married an old friend of Lerner's, Paulette Goddard. One night when the three were having dinner, Lerner jokingly asked Remarque, "How do you get along with this wild woman?"

"Beautifully," Remarque replied. "There is never an argument."

"Never an argument?" Lerner asked incredulously.

"Never," Remarque replied. "We will have an appointment one evening, and she charges into the room crying, 'Why aren't you ready? You always keep me waiting. Why do you...?!' I look at her with astonishment and say, 'Paulette! Who did your hair? It's absolutely ravishing.' She says, 'Really? Do you really like it?' 'Like it?' I reply. You're a vision. Let me see the back.' By the time she has made a pirouette, her fury is forgotten.

"Another time she turns on me in rage about something, and before a sentence is out of her mouth I stare at her and say breathlessly, 'My God! You're incredible. You get younger every day.' She says, 'Really, darling?' 'Tonight,' I say, 'you look eighteen years old.' And that is the end of her rage."

An amused and admiring Lerner said to Remarque: "Erich, one day I will have to write a song about that."

The song was "How to Handle a Woman" which ends:

"The way to handle a woman is to love her, Simply love her; merely love her, Love her, love her."

That's not a bad strategy to deal with anyone.

"Sometimes, you need someone else to believe in you before you believe in yourself," I used to tell my students. "I believe in all of you. They only give me the best and the brightest, and that's why you're in my class."

Successful leaders realize that what most people crave is affirmation. When we affirm them, we reveal our belief in them. And it's amazing how powerful belief can be.

— CHAPTER TWENTY-ONE —

res·ig·na·tion
/ˌrezəgˈnāSH(ə)n/

noun
1. an act of retiring or giving up a position.
2. the acceptance of something undesirable but inevitable.

> *"Humility is not thinking less of yourself.*
> *It's thinking of yourself less."*
> — C.S. Lewis

Perhaps one of the best lessons leaders can learn is how to become more humble and patient. When we resign ourselves to the fact that the universe does not revolve around us, we have taken an important step on our path to discovering greatness.

When I was in high school, my mother decided our family was going to host a foreign exchange student.

No one else in our family had been consulted. Mom just thought it would be a good idea for us to have a stranger from another country living with us for a year, and he would share my bedroom!

Well, we attended a picnic with other families hosting foreign exchange students. There were perhaps 15 families in all, and the new foreign exchange students had a chance to meet their families and mingle with everyone present. I had decided that I was annoyed to have to share my room with a kid from Portugal for the year, so I was not the most sociable person that night.

All of a sudden, though, I saw Holly Van Cleave. She was one of the prettiest and most popular girls at my school. Her family, too, would be hosting a foreign exchange student for the year. With one glance, my entire attitude had changed.

And then, as if by Divine Intervention, I saw her notice me and begin to approach me. I quickly sucked in my gut, brushed my teeth with my tongue and did my best to look as dashing as possible. Holly was actually going to speak to me!

She smiled, extended her hand and asked, "So, what country are you from?"

Well, needless to say, I was crushed. Here I had thought I was "all that," and it turned out that the most popular girl in school didn't even realize we were classmates!

I learned a good lesson from that experience: don't think too highly of yourself. We're all just blips on the radar. Life is short, so it's a good idea to stay humble, and have fun.

⋯⋯⋯⋯⋯●⋯⋯⋯⋯⋯

We all need to be reminded that outward progress doesn't necessarily reflect or measure inward progress. Speaker Zig Ziglar used to tell the story of the Chinese bamboo tree.

When this particular seed of the Chinese bamboo tree is planted, watered and nurtured, for years it doesn't outwardly grow as much as an inch.

Nothing happens for the first year. There's no sign of growth. Not even a hint.

The same thing happens – or doesn't happen – the second year. And then the third year.

The tree is carefully watered and fertilized each year, but nothing shows. No growth. No anything.

So it goes, as the sun rises and sets for four solid years. The farmer and his wife have nothing tangible to show for their labor or effort.

Then, along comes year five.

After five years of fertilizing and watering have passed, with nothing to show for it – the bamboo tree suddenly sprouts and grows 80 feet in just six weeks!

Now, did the little tree lie dormant for four years only to grow exponentially in the fifth?

Or, was the little tree growing underground, developing a root system strong enough to support its potential for outward growth in the fifth year and beyond?

The answer is, of course, obvious.

Had the tree not developed a strong unseen foundation, it could not have sustained its life as it grew.

The founder of Panasonic, Konosuke Matsushita, created a 250-year business plan for his company. When asked what it took to pursue such a long-term philosophy, he offered a one-word answer: "patience."

Your dreams, no matter how big, are not in vain.

Just because you don't see signs of progress now, do not grow weary in continuing to build and give it everything you have – your heart and soul. Even though overly critical friends remind you of how much easier it would be to give up, be more realistic, be more practical or find a new passion, choose to believe that growth is happening underground.

A root system is being formed within your life – the kind of roots that will outlast storms because of the hard work and commitment it has taken to stand in faith for something that cannot be easily proven or qualified. As "they" say, patience is a virtue.

Successful leaders resign themselves to the process.

They are patient.

They are humble.

They *believe*.

— CHAPTER TWENTY-TWO —

ex·pec·ta·tion
/ˌekspekˈtāSH(ə)n/

noun
1. a strong belief that something will happen or be the case in the future.
2. a belief that someone will or should achieve something.

> *"Our environment — the world in which we live and work — is a mirror of our attitudes and expectations."*
> *— Earl Nightingale*

Do you ever feel discouraged, like the whole world is collapsing?

One of the pleasures of reading is finding positive stories to inspire me. I came across one in the newspaper recently that warmed my heart and renewed my faith in humanity.

The story read:

> In the predawn hours of a Saturday morning in January, an arsonist set fire to the Victoria Islamic Center, a mosque in Victoria, Texas. The fire gutted the building, but the shocked community immediately responded with love and kindness. The Jewish and Christian communities of Victoria quickly stepped up, offering their churches and a synagogue for worship to the congregation of fewer than 150 people. And within days, a GoFundMe account set up to raise funds for rebuilding the uninsured structure surpassed the goal of $850,000, raising more than $1 million from people of all beliefs – including atheists.

Negative news sells, but positive news soothes.

Do yourself a favor and stay away from the screaming commentators on television and cryptic correspondents in print. Avoid politicians who lead by fear. Focus your attention on the positives, and you will be astounded how it restores your faith.

Expect the best, and you'll be amazed what ensues.

· · · · · · · · · ● · · · · · · · · · ·

Not sold on people? Well, then, turn to nature for inspiration.

We can learn a lot from geese. I read some amazing facts about their habits, and it got me thinking about what we can learn from their example.

In the fall, when you see geese heading South for the winter – flying along in a V formation – you might consider what science has discovered as to why they fly that way:

As each bird flaps its wings, it creates an uplift for the bird immediately following. By flying in V formation, the whole flock adds at least 71% greater flying range than if each bird flew on its own.

Wouldn't you agree that people who share a common direction and sense of community can get where they are going more quickly and easily because they are traveling on the thrust of one another?

When a goose falls out of formation, it suddenly feels the drag and resistance trying to go it alone and quickly gets back into formation to take advantage of the lifting power of the bird in front.

Isn't it wise to stay in formation with those who are headed in the same direction as we are?

When the head goose gets tired, it rotates back in the wing, and another goose flies point.

Don't you think it is sensible to take turns doing demanding jobs – with people or with geese flying South?

Geese honk from behind to encourage those up front to keep up their speed.

Isn't it a good idea to support those making progress to continue?

Finally – and this is important – when a goose gets sick or is wounded by gunshots and falls out of formation, two other geese fall out with that goose and follow it down to lend help and protection. They stay with the fallen goose until it is able to fly or until it dies – and only then do they launch out on their own, or with another formation to catch up with their group.

If we have the sense of geese, we can more easily recognize the potential benefits of collaborative and integrated efforts. When leaders create environments where everyone is expected to help one another to lift the entire group, it's amazing what happens.

What expectations have you set with your team?

· · · · · · · · · · ● · · · · · · · · · · ·

We tend to get what we think we'll get.

In his terrific book *It's Not What You Sell, It's What You Stand For*, author and advertising executive Roy Spence argues that nobody exemplified the power of high expectations better than Wal-Mart founder Sam Walton.

When a reporter asked a representative from Sears about the threat posed by Wal-Mart spreading around the country – all the way into the hometown of the Sears headquarters in Chicago – the Sears representative belittled the man who would eventually become the wealthiest person in the world.

"We're going to send that squirrel hunter right back to Arkansas," he boasted. "The discount concept won't fly in the big city."

What Walton understood – and many less successful people fail to grasp – is that when you've found the thrill and the will, and your team members, employees or colleagues share that passion, don't be afraid to set audacious goals that seem unrealistic to your critics and competitors.

Spence shares another anecdote about Walton recounted by Don Sonderquist, the retired chief operating officer and vice chairman of Wal-Mart:

> [In the early 1970s] there was a group of eight small regional discount store chains whose executives met several times a year to share ideas on how to improve operations. None

of their stores were in competition with each other, as they were in different geographical locations.

At the end of one of those meetings in 1972, one of the CEOs thought it would be interesting to hear what each thought his company sales would be in ten years. The first CEO said that his sales were at $40 million in the past year, and he believed that they could move them up to $80 million in a decade. The next said that his company's sales were $60 million, and he expected to be at $100 million in ten years. Another said that sales were already $100 million, and he believed his stores could reach $160 million in that period.

Finally, Sam said that Wal-Mart sales were at $44 million, and he expected that in ten years they would reach $2 billion. Everyone laughed. What they didn't understand at the time was that Sam was serious. Ten years later, Wal-Mart sales exceeded $2 billion.

Sam Walton modeled the power of high expectations. On a mission to save people money so they could live better, he gave himself permission to think big.

Leaders understand the power of expectations. To paraphrase Henry Ford: whether you believe you can or can't – you're right.

— CHAPTER TWENTY-THREE —

tol·er·a·tion
/ˌtälə'rāSH(ə)n/

noun
1. the practice of tolerating something, in particular differences of opinion or behavior.
2. the act of allowing something.

> *"Criticism is something we can avoid easily by saying nothing, doing nothing, and being nothing."*
> *— Aristotle*

President Theodore "Teddy" Roosevelt knew a thing or two about keeping an open mind. He was a constant student since his childhood. Indeed, even as President, he is said to have read at least three books a day.

Still, Roosevelt had his share of critics.

Some argued that he over-stepped his authority with his "generous" use of executive orders (he issued over 1,000; by contrast, his predecessor – President McKinley – had only issued around 100). He also used his power to create the United States Forest Service in order to protect wildlife and public lands. Perhaps most shocking was his audacity to invite Booker T. Washington, a former slave, to the White House for dinner, during a time when segregation was the law in the United States.

After leaving office, President Roosevelt delivered a speech in Paris on April 23, 1910, that would become one of the most widely-quoted speeches of his illustrious career.

"The poorest way to face life is to face it with a sneer," he said, admonishing his critics. "A cynical habit of thought and speech, a readiness to criticize work which the critic himself never tries to perform, an intellectual aloofness which will not accept contact with life's realities – all these are marks, not...of superiority, but of weakness."

The President did not stop there. He continued, to huge applause:

> It is not the critic who counts; not the man who points out how the strong man stumbles, or where the doer of deeds could have done them better. The credit belongs to the man who is actually in the arena, whose face is

marred by dust and sweat and blood; who strives valiantly; who errs, who comes short again and again, because there is no effort without error and shortcoming; but who does actually strive to do the deeds; who knows great enthusiasms, the great devotions; who spends himself in a worthy cause; who at best knows in the end the triumph of high achievement, and who at the worst, if he fails, at least fails while daring greatly, so that his place shall never be with these cold and timid souls who neither know victory nor defeat.

All leaders face challenges.

All leaders have their critics.

The best leaders manage to tolerate their critics and keep an open mind.

· · · · · · · · · · · ● · · · · · · · · · · · ·

There's a quote that goes:

We all operate in two contrasting modes, which might be called open and closed. The open mode is more relaxed, more receptive, more exploratory, more democratic, more playful and more humorous. The closed mode is tighter, more rigid, more hierarchical, more tunnel-visioned. Most people, unfortunately, spend most of their time in the closed mode.

The gentleman who said this would know a thing or two about open-mindedness versus closed-mindedness, as he has endured his share of criticism over his career.

He was tall and lanky from a young age. One critic said the gentleman's performances reminded him of an accountant.

The "accountant" studied law at Cambridge but wound up earning a healthy income as a writer and performer.

When he joined forces with other friends from Cambridge and Oxford, they created a unique television show.

The BBC head of light entertainment failed to see the show as funny.

Their form of humor prevailed, however, earning them millions of fans around the world.

They called their comedy troupe "Monty Python," and the "unfunny accountant" was John Cleese, who has managed to keep a fairly open mind throughout his career as one of the most beloved comedians around the world.

— CHAPTER TWENTY-FOUR —

in·spi·ra·tion
/ˌinspəˈrāSH(ə)n/

noun
1. the process of being mentally stimulated to do or feel something, especially to do something creative.
2. a sudden brilliant, creative, or timely idea.

> "*Act as if what you do makes a difference...It does.*"
> – William James

Inspiration is all around us. You just have to look for it.

In the days when an ice cream sundae cost much less, a 10-year-old boy entered a hotel coffee shop and sat at a table. A waitress put a glass of water in front of him.

"How much is an ice cream sundae?" the boy inquired.

"50 cents," replied the waitress.

The little boy pulled his hand out of his pocket and studied a number of coins in it.

"How much is a dish of plain ice cream?" he asked.

Some people were now waiting for a table, and the waitress was a bit impatient with her juvenile customer.

"35 cents," she said brusquely.

The little boy again counted the coins.

"I'll have the plain ice cream," he said.

The waitress brought the ice cream, put the bill on the table and walked away. The boy finished the ice cream, paid the cashier and departed.

When the waitress returned to the boy's table, she began wiping it down. She then swallowed hard at what she saw.

There, placed neatly beside the empty dish, were 15 cents – her tip.

In the military, there's a concept known as "leave no man behind." Soldiers are trained to work together and depend on one another. Words like "duty" and "loyalty" have significant meaning.

Friendship and camaraderie are precious commodities, so I love to read about acts of selflessness from around the world in business and in life throughout history.

Take Zanjeer, a loyal servant of the Mumbai police department. In his police career, Zanjeer detected more than 3,329 kilograms of explosive RDX, 600 detonators, 249 hand grenades, and 6,406 rounds of live ammunition, saving thousands of lives. When he passed away from cancer, his colleagues awarded him a hero's funeral.

In 1903, Bud accompanied Dr. Horatio Nelson Jackson on the first automobile journey from coast to coast. In just sixty-three and a half days, the two bravely journeyed from San Francisco to New York city, well before highways and service stations changed the American landscape forever.

A veteran of 17 battles on the Western Front, "Stubby" was a soldier in the Yankee Division of the 102nd Infantry. He learned to detect dangerous mustard gas and would scout for wounded colleagues between battles. His brothers-in-arms also credited him as being an early warning system for bombings and raids.

And no discussion of loyalty and friendship could be complete without mentioning Hachiko, who met the evening train every day for nine years, nine months and 15 days, patiently waiting for his friend who (unbeknownst to him) had passed away.

While living in different parts of the world and serving in their own ways, Zanjeer, Bud, Stubby and Hachiko shared a common characteristic: they all lived up to the moniker "man's best friend," as all were dogs.

See, leaders come in all shapes and sizes – and even species, it would seem.

CHAPTER TWENTY-FIVE

de·ter·mi·na·tion
/dəˌtərməˈnāSH(ə)n/

noun
1. firmness of purpose; resoluteness.
2. the process of establishing something exactly by calculation or research.

> "I ran and ran and ran every day, and I acquired this sense of determination, this sense of spirit that I would never, never give up, no matter what else happened."
> — Wilma Rudolph

One day, on the plains of Africa, a young water buffalo named Walter approached his dad and asked him if there was anything that he should be afraid of.

"Only lions, my son," his dad responded.

"Oh yes, I've heard about lions. If I ever see one, I'll turn and run as fast as I can," said Walter.

"No, that's the worst thing you can do," said his father.

"Why? They are scary and will try to kill me."

The dad smiled and explained, "Walter, if you run away, the lions will chase you and catch you. And when they do, they will jump on your unprotected back and bring you down."

"So what should I do?" asked Walter.

"If you ever see a lion, stand your ground to show him that you're not afraid. If he doesn't move away, show him your sharp horns and stomp the ground with your hooves. If that doesn't work, move slowly towards him.

And if that doesn't work, charge him and hit him with everything you've got!"

"That's crazy, I'll be too scared to do that," replied the startled young water buffalo. "What if he attacks me back?"

"Look around, Walter. What do you see?"

Walter looked around at the rest of his herd. There were about 200 massive beasts – all armed with sharp horns and huge shoulders.

"If ever you're afraid, know that we are here. If you panic and run from your fears, we can't save you, but if you charge towards them, we'll be right behind you."

The young water buffalo breathed deeply and nodded. "Thanks, Dad," he said. "I think I understand." We all have lions in our worlds. There are aspects of life that scare us and make us want to run, but if we do, they will chase us down and take over our lives. Our thoughts will become dominated by the things that we are afraid of, and our actions will become timid and cautious, not allowing us to reach our full potential.

In the Bible, it says in James 4:7, "Resist the devil, and he will flee from you."

Courage does not mean a lack of fear. Leaders face their fears – determined to succeed, in spite of being afraid.

· · · · · · · · · · ◉ · · · · · · · · · · ·

It's nice to be talented, but the old saying is true: "Hard work beats talent when talent doesn't work hard."

Despite their obvious gifts, successful people wouldn't be where they are today without having insane work ethics.

Apple CEO Tim Cook routinely begins emailing employees at 4:30 in the morning. He's typically the first in the office and the last to leave. He even used to hold staff meetings on Sunday nights in order to prepare for the upcoming week.

At first glance, Dallas Mavericks owner Mark Cuban's amazing success looks like a stroke of luck, as he sold his first company at the peak of its value and got into technology stocks at exactly the right time. A closer look reveals that when starting that first company, he routinely stayed up until 2 a.m. reading about new software and went seven years without a vacation.

Venus and Serena Williams, who between them have won 30 Grand Slam singles championships in tennis, were all but raised on the court. Their sister Isha described their daily routine growing up as: "Get up – 6 o'clock in the morning, go to the tennis court, before school. After school, go to tennis."

By age 15, Li Ka-Shing had left school and was working in a plastics factory. He quickly became a salesman, outsold everybody else and became the factory's general manager by 19. In 1950, he started his own plastics business and did almost everything, including the accounting, himself. Today he is one of the richest men in Asia, with an empire valued at over $31 billion.

While putting herself through Yale, Indra Nooyi worked the graveyard shift as a receptionist. Throughout her career she typically woke up at 4 a.m., and at times in her career it was normal for her to work until midnight. Today she is one of the most powerful and well-known women in business, rising in the ranks all the way to becoming the CEO of Pepsi.

Businessman and author Harvey Mackay said, "I've known successful sales people who were drunks, gamblers, liars, and thieves...but I have never known a successful sales person who sat on his (butt) all day." Remember: success is not handed to you. It is earned. Leaders understand that they must put in the work.

CHAPTER TWENTY-SIX

in·no·va·tion

/ˌinəˈvāSH(ə)n/

noun
1. the action or process of innovating.
2. a new method, idea, product, etc.

> *"The difficulty lies not so much in developing new ideas as in escaping from old ones."*
> — John Maynard Keynes

Leaders innovate.

By the late 1800s, large cities all around the world were "drowning in horse manure." In order for these cities to function, they were dependent on thousands of horses for the transport of both people and goods.

This huge number of horses created major problems.

The main concern was the large amount of manure left behind on the streets, as a horse would produce an average of between 15 and 35 pounds of manure per day. The manure on city streets also attracted huge numbers of flies that spread typhoid fever and other diseases.

Each horse also produced around two pints of urine per day, and - to make things worse - the average life expectancy for a working horse was only around three years. Horse carcasses had to be removed from the streets, but the bodies were often left to putrefy so the corpses could be more easily sawn into pieces for removal.

Public streets were literally beginning to poison people, and the crisis became known as "The Great Manure Crisis of 1894."

Solutions to the terrible situation were offered at the world's first international urban planning conference in New York in 1898, but no solution could be found.

It seemed society was doomed.

One man solved the "impossible" problem. His name was Henry Ford.

Ford came up with a process of building "automobiles" at affordable prices. Cars and buses soon replaced horse-drawn carriages as the main source

of transport, and by 1912, the seemingly insurmountable problem had been resolved.

What is "impossible" for you?

............●............

The first major polio epidemic in the United States
occurred in Vermont in the summer of 1894, and –
by the early 1900s – thousands were affected every
year. Since the virus is easily transmitted, epidemics
were commonplace.

At the beginning of the 20th century, treatments for
the virus were limited to quarantines and the infa-
mous "iron lung," a metal coffin-like contraption that
aided respiration. Children – especially infants –
were among the worst affected by the terrifying
disease.

Adults were also afflicted with the disease – none
more famous than future President Franklin Delano
Roosevelt, who was stricken with the disease at the
age of 39 and left partially paralyzed. He would later
transform his estate in Warm Springs, Georgia, into a
recovery retreat center for polio victims, and he was
also instrumental in raising funds for polio-related
research and treatment.

Over 58,000 new cases of polio were reported in
1952 – an epidemic year for polio. Tragically, more
than 3,000 died from the disease that year. But on

March 26th, 1953, Dr. Jonas Salk – an American medical researcher and virologist – announced that he had successfully tested a vaccine against polio-myelitis, the virus that causes polio.

This first successful polio vaccine, known as inactivated poliovirus vaccine (IPV) or "Salk vaccine," contained the killed virus and was administered by injection to patients. In 1954, clinical trials using the vaccine and a placebo began on nearly two million American school children. The vaccine was announced to be safe and effective in 1955, the same year the vaccination was licensed, leading to the wide distribution of the vaccine to children in the United States.

After the National Foundation for Infantile Paralysis promoted a nationwide inoculation campaign, the annual number of polio cases fell from 35,000 in 1953 to 5,600 by 1957. By 1961 only 161 cases were recorded in the United States.

Today, there are just a handful of polio cases annually in the United States, and most of these are "imported" by immigrants from developing nations where polio is still a problem.

Among a slew of other honors, Salk was awarded the Presidential Medal of Freedom – the nation's highest civilian honor – in 1977.

If there is one thing that leaders have proven over the years, it is that no obstacle is insurmountable. Indeed, greater urgency tends to stimulate innovation quicker.

CHAPTER TWENTY-SEVEN

con·sid·er·a·tion
/kən͵sidərˈāSH(ə)n/

noun
1. careful thought, typically over a period
    of time.

> "The best and most beautiful things in the world cannot be
> seen or even touched — they must be felt with the heart."
> – Helen Keller

Have you ever heard of Miep Gies? Probably not.

Following the rise of Adolf Hitler and the Nazi party in 1933, the Jewish Frank family decided to escape to the Netherlands to flee the rapidly escalating anti-Semitism in Germany. Otto and Edith Frank, along with their daughters Margot and Anne, went into hiding in an annex above Otto's offices in

Amsterdam on July 6th, 1942. Four other Jews soon joined them.

The family was helped into hiding by a number of people who had worked for Otto Frank, including Miep Gies, who had started work as an office assistant for Frank in 1933. During the two years and 35 days the Frank family lived in the secret annex, Gies (along with other helpers) visited frequently with food and other supplies, and shared news from the outside.

Above all, the friendship and kindness shown by Gies proved a lifeline for Anne, who kept a diary about her experiences and thoughts while in hiding.

On August 4th, 1944, everyone in the annex was arrested. Somebody had called the German Security Police to notify them that Jews were in hiding at Prinsengracht 263. The identity of the caller has never been established. Everyone in the annex was deported – first to the Westerbork transit camp, and then on to Auschwitz.

In the autumn of 1944, Anne and her sister Margot were transported to Bergen-Belsen, a concentration camp in Germany where almost 4,000 Jews, primarily Dutch, were imprisoned. There, facing unsanitary conditions and having no food, the girls contracted typhus. They both died in March 1945, just a few weeks before the camp was liberated.

After the family's arrest, Gies discovered Anne's diary and kept it, unread, hoping she could one day return it to Anne. Sadly, this never happened, and she instead gave it to Otto – the only member of the family to survive the war, in July of 1945.

"I began to read slowly, only a few pages each day, more would have been impossible, as I was overwhelmed by painful memories," Otto later recalled. "For me, it was a revelation. There was revealed a completely different Anne to the child that I had lost. I had no idea of the depths of her thoughts and feelings."

Very few remember Miep Gies, but Anne Frank's diary was published in the Netherlands on June 25th, 1947. It remains one of the most famous – and best-selling – books of all time. And it was made possible by the kindness of Miep Gies.

So, how can you be a little kinder today? You never know: one small act of kindness can change the world.

· · · · · · · · · ● · ● · · · · · · · · · ·

I say a prayer before I go on stages to speak. Basically, I ask God to use me as an instrument to inspire others. There's a neat line in the Bible (Ephesians 5:1) where the apostle Paul writes, "Be imitators of God, as beloved children, and live in love, as Christ loved us."

Loving one another without judgment is something all of us could do a little more, but I often wondered what it means to live in love. Then I heard the story of Tony Campolo.

Tony had a hard time sleeping one night, so he got up at 3:30 a.m. and went searching for an all-night coffee shop. He found one and ordered a donut and a cup of coffee – when two prostitutes came in. They were loud and crude and quite disagreeable company. Tony was ready to leave when he over-heard one of the women say that the next day was her birthday.

Her friend sneered, "So what do you want from me? A birthday party?" To which the woman replied, "Why should you give me a birthday party? I've never had a birthday party in my whole life."

Now, when Tony heard that, something clicked in-side. He went over to the waiter and asked if the women came in every night. The waiter said they did. Then Tony asked if he could hold a birthday party for the one woman, Agnes. The waiter thought it was a wonderful idea and agreed.

Tony was back at the diner the next night at 2:30 a.m. to decorate. He brought some crepe-paper dec-orations and made a big birthday sign out of pieces of cardboard. He covered that diner from one end to the other. Somehow word of the party must have gotten out, because pretty soon the diner began to fill up with friends of Agnes.

At 3:30, Agnes and the other woman entered the diner. Everyone shouted, "Happy Birthday, Agnes!" and began singing "Happy Birthday."

Well, Agnes was stunned. Her mouth fell wide open. By the time the waiter brought in the cake she was crying.

A little later Tony led the group in prayer.

Now, anyone who can read this story without shedding a tear is much stronger than I'll ever be. When I think about how Tony Campolo looked at this woman as another human being and treated her with such dignity and kindness, it was a wake-up call.

How many other people are there out in the world like Agnes who have never been shown a bit of kindness? Or shown the least bit of gratitude? Or given a birthday party?

There is so much darkness in the world, and yet any one of us can lead others to new heights – often with just the simplest consideration.

— CHAPTER TWENTY-EIGHT —

sal·va·tion

/salˈvāSH(ə)n/

noun

1. preservation or deliverance from harm,
    ruin, or loss.

> *"A well-developed sense of humor is the pole that adds*
> *balance to your steps as you walk the tightrope of life."*
> — William Arthur Ward

Do the people around you *contribute* to your joy,
prosperity and freedom...or do they *contaminate*
them?

Life is tough. People are thrown all sorts of curve-
balls – extraordinary highs and debilitating lows...joy
and happiness, pain and suffering.

Life is also too short to take yourself too seriously. Laughter is the best medicine. Humor is salvation during tough or trying times, and the most effective leaders know how to laugh at themselves.

One of the pleasures of teaching children – especially young children – is that they constantly cause me to laugh and think, as they see the world in different ways.

I attended a number of different Catholic schools during my elementary years (we can discuss at a later date why I attended a *number* of them). At one particular school, all of us kids lined up in the cafeteria for lunch one day.

At the head of the table was a large pile of apples. Sister Karen had made a note and posted it on the apple tray. It said, "Take only one. God is watching."

Moving further along the lunch line, at the other end of the table was a large pile of chocolate chip cookies. One of my classmates, Casey, had written a note. It said, "Take all you want. God's watching the apples."

· · · · · · · · · ● · · · · · · · · · ·

A bishop invited a young priest to dinner.

During the meal, the priest noticed some signs of intimacy between the bishop and his housekeeper.

As the priest was leaving, the bishop said to him quietly, "I can guess what you are thinking, but really our relationship is strictly proper."

A few days later the housekeeper remarked to the bishop that a valuable antique solid silver soup ladle was missing – since the young priest's visit – and so she wondered if he might have taken it.

"I doubt it, but I will ask him," said the bishop.

So the bishop wrote to the priest: "Dear Father, I am not saying that 'you did' take a solid silver ladle from my house, and I am not saying that 'you did not' take a solid silver ladle from my house, but the fact is that the ladle has been missing since your visit."

Duly, the bishop received the young priest's reply, which read: "Your Excellency, I'm not saying that 'you do' sleep with your housekeeper, and I'm not saying that 'you do not' sleep with your housekeeper, but the fact is that if you were sleeping in your own bed, you would by now have found the ladle."

· · · · · · · · · · ● · · · · · · · · · · ·

A shepherd was tending his flock in a field, when a new sports car screeched to a stop on the road nearby in a cloud of dust. The driver, a young man in expensive designer clothes and sunglasses, leaned out of the window and shouted over to the shepherd,

"If I tell you exactly how many sheep you have here, can I take one?"

The shepherd looked up slowly at the young man, then looked at his peaceful flock and calmly answered, "Sure, why not?"

The young man stepped out of his car holding a brand-new smart phone, with which he proceeded to connect to a series of websites – first calling up the satellite navigation system to pinpoint his location, then keying in the location to generate an ultra-high-resolution picture of the field. After emailing the photo to an image-processing facility, he soon received the processed data, which he then fed into an online database and entered the parameters for a report. Within another few seconds a miniature printer in the car produced a full-color report containing several pages of analysis and results. The young man studied the data for a few more seconds and returned to the shepherd.

"You have exactly 1,586 sheep, including three rams – and 722 lambs."

"That's right," said the shepherd, mildly impressed. "Well, I guess that means you get to take one of my sheep."

The young man made his choice and loaded the animal onto the backseat of his car.

"Hey there," the shepherd said, almost as an afterthought. "If I can tell you what your business is, will you give me back my sheep?"

Feeling confident, the young man readily agreed.

"You're a consultant," said the shepherd.

"Wow, that's right," said the young man, taken aback. "How did you guess that?"

"No guessing required," the shepherd replied. "You showed up here, even though nobody called you. You took a fee for giving me an answer that I already knew, to a question I never asked and you know nothing about my business. Now give me back my dog."

See, life is too short to be grumpy and bitter. We each have daily choices: what to read, who to hang out with, etc. Surround yourself with positives, and you'll find life to be a lot more rewarding.

CHAPTER TWENTY-NINE

im·ag·i·na·tion
/i͵majəˈnāSH(ə)n/

noun
1. the faculty or action of forming new ideas, or images or concepts of external objects not present to the senses.
2. the ability of the mind to be creative or resourceful.

> *"An invasion of armies can be resisted, but not an idea whose time has come."*
> – Victor Hugo

How creative are you?

Once a well-dressed Russian businessman walked into a Swiss bank in Geneva and asked for a loan of 100 Swiss francs. He offered his luxury Mercedes car as collateral. The collateral was too good to refuse, and the bank manager readily approved the loan.

A year later, the Russian returned. He repaid the banker the loan plus the 10% interest and was ready to collect his car. Finally, the puzzled bank manager dared to ask: "Excuse me, sir, could you tell me: did you really need the 100 Swiss francs so badly? In order to get the money, you left your luxury car with us for an entire year!"

The Russian smiled. "That's simple," he replied. "Where else in Geneva could I have found such a great parking place for just 10 Swiss francs a year?"'

See, some of our most clever ideas emerge when we let our creative juices flow. What can you do to encourage more creativity each day?

· · · · · · · · · ● ● ● · · · · · · · · · ·

A lady took her adorable little pet Chihuahua with her on a safari holiday.

Wandering too far one day, the Chihuahua got lost in the bush, where he soon encountered a very hungry-looking leopard. Realizing the danger, the Chihuahua began to retreat when he noticed some fresh bones on the ground.

With his back to the big cat, the shrewd little dog settled down to chew on the bones. And just before the leopard leapt on him – in what certainly would have meant his fatal end, the Chihuahua smacked his lips loudly and exclaimed, "Boy, that was one delicious leopard! I wonder if there are any more around here?"

Hearing this, the leopard stopped mid-stride and retreated back into the forest.

"Phew, that was close," said the leopard. "That evil little dog nearly had me!"

A monkey nearby watched everything and thought he'd win a favor by setting the stupid leopard straight. When the Chihuahua saw the monkey trail the leopard, he quickly surmised that the monkey was up to no good.

After hearing the monkey's story, the leopard felt humiliated and angry at being made a fool. So he offered the monkey a ride back to see him exact his revenge on the clever canine.

As the Chihuahua saw them approach, he feared the worse. Thinking quickly, he turned his back again and pretended not to notice the leopard and his monkey informant.

When the pair were within earshot, the Chihuahua loudly announced, "Now, where's that monkey gone to? I sent him ages ago to bring me another leopard to eat."

Creativity comes in many forms.

And creative ideas can come from anywhere.

A philosophy professor gave an unusual test to his class. He lifted his chair onto his desk and wrote on the board simply: "Prove that this chair does not exist."

The class set to work, composing long complex explanations – except one student.

One young lady took just thirty seconds to complete and hand in her paper, attracting surprised glances from her classmates and the professor.

The following week the class received their grades for the test. The student who took thirty seconds was judged the best.

Her answer was, "What chair?"

Japanese grocery stores had a problem.

They are much smaller than shops in the United States and therefore don't have room to waste. Watermelons, big and round, wasted a lot of space. Most people would simply tell the grocery stores that watermelons grow round and there is nothing that can be done about it.

That is how the majority of people would respond.

But some Japanese farmers took a different approach.

If the supermarkets wanted a square watermelon, they asked themselves, "How can we provide one?"

It wasn't long before they invented the square watermelon.

Japanese farmers solved the problem of the round watermelons because they did not assume it was impossible. Instead, they simply asked how it could be done.

They found out that if you put the watermelons in square boxes when they are growing, the watermelons will take on the shape of the boxes and grow into square fruit.

This made the grocery stores happy and had the added benefit that it was much easier and cost-effective to ship the watermelons. Consumers also loved them because they took less space in their refrigerators, which are much smaller than those in the United States. And since they became so popular, growers discovered they could charge a premium price for them.

Effective leaders use the power of imagination to solve problems. By looking at questions from alternative perspectives, they often discover simple, creative solutions. By asking the question, "Is there a better way of doing this," leaders find there often is.

CHAPTER THIRTY

ap·pre·ci·a·tion

/əˌprēSHēˈāSH(ə)n/

noun
1. recognition and enjoyment of the good qualities of someone or something.
2. a full understanding of a situation.

> *"Cherish each hour of this day, for it can never return."*
> — Og Mandino

Have you ever noticed that most of the people who advise others to "enjoy the journey" have already experienced massive success? It is difficult to imagine that those same people showed appreciation as they went through their trials and tribulations.

I'd like to be tan, trim and wealthy and admonish others to "enjoy the journey." Unfortunately, my journey is a work in progress, as I'm pale, overweight and could use a raise as much as the next person.

It's hard to succeed. That's why not everyone does.

There are so many opportunities to quit. At any given time most people find it easy to make excuses about why things may not be going their way. Indeed, how often do you actually look like your social media picture?

It's easy to ignore the little things. Enjoying the journey, on the other hand, is hard work.

I'm not happy when I see my business partner losing money, as he invests in opportunities he thinks will grow our business, only to find out they were scams or wasted energy. Being a parent to three children is wonderful, but I have not always enjoyed their temper tantrums or sleepless nights or trips to the emergency room. And as much as I love speaking around the world, I cannot say I am enjoying the journey when my flight's delayed, my rental car breaks down, the sheets on my motel bed look like they were last washed eight guests ago and my best dining options await in a vending machine.

What does it take to really enjoy the journey? A sense of humor. Someday I hope to meet my maker and hear God howl as he pats me on the back and recounts all of my "miseries" throughout life. A little perspective can go a long way. I have a beautiful, healthy family. I am typing this on a laptop that I am blessed to own. And every now and then, when I am lucky, someone – often a stranger – writes me a kind email to tell me how much they enjoy one of my books.

Yes, at the end of the day, after I re-run the "woe is me" parts of my day, it is truly delightful to sit in silence and relish all of the blessings I so often take for granted.

So I implore you to enjoy your journey, and share your trials and tribulations with others, as *all* of us can relate.

· · · · · · · · · ● · · · · · · · · · · ·

A heart surgeon took his car to his local garage for a regular service, where he usually exchanged a little friendly banter with the owner, a skilled but not especially wealthy mechanic.

"So tell me," the mechanic said. "I've been wondering about what we both do for a living, and how much more you get paid than me."

"Yes?" the surgeon answered.

"Well, look at this," said the mechanic, as he worked on a big complicated engine. "I check how it's running, open it up, fix the valves and put it all back together so it works good as new. We basically do the same job don't we? And yet you are paid ten times what I am - how do you explain that?"

The surgeon thought for a moment, and smiling gently, replied, "Try it with the engine running."

How we value things all depends on our perception. To some, a sports car may have a lot of value. To others, better health may be everything. In the movie *Citizen Kane* a reporter futilely attempted to track down what Charles Foster Kane's dying last words meant. To me, time spent reading with my children is priceless.

What do you appreciate most about every day?

· · · · · · · · ● · · · · · · · · · ·

One of my favorite books is Jules Verne's *Around the World in 80 Days.* To those who don't know, the story follows the escapades of Victorian-era Englishman Phileas Fogg. When he is challenged by his fellow members of a London gentleman's club to prove his contention that a man can circumnavigate the globe in a mere 80 days (remember, this book was written in 1872), Fogg bets his entire fortune and leaves with his stalwart manservant, Passepartout, alongside. Meanwhile, the Bank of England has been robbed, so a determined detective is in hot pursuit as the public is left to wonder if Mr. Fogg's adventure is really a ploy to avoid arrest.

The journey of Phileas Fogg and Passepartout takes them eastward to exotic locales on every imaginable type of transport. In India, they encounter a group of tribal Indians preparing to sacrifice a young woman (Aouda) whose husband, a prince, has just died. They save the princess and bring her along for the remainder of their journey as the British detective is hot on their trail.

Just when it looks like they are going to make it back to London to win the wager, the detective captures them and holds them in jail. Soon, however, the detective learns that the real bank robber was arrested three days before, so he releases Fogg, Passepartout and Aouda so they can make their way to London. Alas, they arrive in London a few minutes too late.

Always a gentleman, Fogg sits alone in his room for a long time. But when Aouda professes her love for him, he is overjoyed and asks for Passepartout to make wedding arrangements for the next day, Monday. While he goes to find the reverend, however, Passepartout discovers that it is not Sunday but Saturday – they had gained a day when crossing the International Date Line! Fogg rushes to his club in time to win the wager, but he believes the greatest reward for his trip was finding Aouda.

What I love about the story is that it reinforces the importance of time. And it reminds us that it truly is the journey, not the destination, that matters most.

Are you enjoying your journey right now? If not, make a change.

Time is precious. We need to cherish every minute we have on this earth.

CHAPTER THIRTY-ONE

cel·e·bra·tion
/ˌseləˈbrāSH(ə)n/

noun
1. the action of marking one's pleasure at an important event or occasion by engaging in enjoyable, typically social, activity.

> *"Celebrate what you've accomplished, but raise the bar a little higher each time you succeed."*
> — Mia Hamm

Ever read the early Harry Potter books? Students at Hogwarts work hard every year. And what happens at the end? They have a grand feast. They celebrate all that they have endured.

Whether you trade stocks, teach students, coach players – whatever – you need to find time to lighten up and celebrate all that you have accomplished. Otherwise, what's the point?

A lot of people praise generals who always focus on the next battle or executives who concentrate solely on the next product that will boost their profits. I pity these people. Everyone needs to step back and acknowledge the fruits of their labor. The person who does not celebrate risks losing balance in other areas of their life.

Former Ohio State football coach Urban Meyer recalls that immediately after he won his second national championship at the University of Florida, he was on the phone speaking with recruits rather than celebrating with his coaches and players. The stress to constantly improve affected Meyer so much that he eventually quit his job for health reasons. Only after making a pact with his family to focus more on family, friends and leisure did he agree to return to the world of college coaching – and to great success.

What do you do to celebrate? How can you make work fun every day? Are your employees fans of your company? Take a moment to think about ways you can celebrate all that you do. Then, do it!

· · · · · · · · · ● ● ● · · · · · · · · ·

We live in a fast-paced world where we are taught that "accomplishment" means getting as much done in a day as you possibly can. However, too many of us don't take the time to reflect on our accomplishments. When was the last time that you stopped and took a moment to celebrate and reward yourself? If you struggle with this notion, you aren't alone.

A young man recently committed suicide at my oldest daughter's high school, and it sparked a lot of soul-searching in our home. I felt so sorry for that boy's family, and it devastated me that a human being could not see his value on this earth. You need to know that the world has never known anyone like you, and it never will again. Don't wait for others to recognize your value; God already sees it! You need to pause and celebrate yourself every day.

If you are constantly *doing* and not *being*, you will miss out on all the beautiful moments in life. Remember: you are a human being, not a human doing.

Oftentimes, we take life too seriously, and we become so attached to the final outcome that we forget to enjoy the journey. Don't get me wrong: it's great to be ambitious. However, the key is to develop a mindset that allows you to pursue big things in life, without sacrificing the small things that make life worth living.

Take a moment every day, stop what you are doing, savor the moment and celebrate.

Many of us have limiting beliefs about ourselves in at least one area of our lives, and this results in a decrease in confidence. The more that you celebrate yourself, the more your confidence boosts. And this, in turn, attracts more positive energy into your life.

So don't ever hold back. Be proud of who you are and what you have accomplished. You step into your power when you are able to master this skill. Are you ready to take ownership of your amazingness?

When you take time every day to acknowledge the little actions that you are taking towards the achievement of your goals, you strengthen those actions. In what ways can you acknowledge yourself today? Take a moment and think about what you have accomplished. Heck, congratulate yourself for something as simple as finishing this sentence!

To love yourself means to celebrate the very existence of who you are. Hold yourself in high regard. You deserve it.

CHAPTER THIRTY-TWO

fix·a·tion
/fikˈsāSH(ə)n/

noun
1. an obsessive interest in or feeling about someone or something.

> "Concentrate all your thoughts upon the work at hand. The sun's rays do not burn until brought to a focus."
> — Alexander Graham Bell

In 1948 in the southern California city of San Bernardino, the McDonald brothers were introducing the world to its fast-food hamburgers. That same year, though, newlyweds Harry and Esther Snyder founded their own hamburger shop down the road in Baldwin Park – about 45 miles away.

And while the McDonald brothers focused on speed, lower prices and franchising, the Snyders focused on a simple menu, fresh ingredients and "family" ownership.

The Snyders introduced an innovation that would impact the entire emerging "fast food" industry: an outdoor, two-way speaker box connected to the restaurant's kitchen – allowing diners to order their meals in their cars in one of the nation's first "drive-thrus." And when the drive-thru lines would get especially long, employees would run outside and take orders directly from customers.

While their competitors have heavily invested in massive advertising campaigns, franchise expansion and expanded menu offerings, the Snyder family business remains much as it did during the life of its co-founder, Harry Snyder. For over 70 years, they have offered customers a simple menu: cooked-to-order hamburgers crafted from fresh ground beef – topped with fresh produce and served on freshly baked buns. Patrons can watch employees hand-cut French fries from real potatoes in front of them in the restaurant's open kitchen – also one of the first in the fast-food industry – and wash down their meals with milkshakes made from real ice cream.

By the time of Harry's passing in 1976, the Snyders owned restaurants at 18 locations. Son Rich grew the business to 93 outlets by the time of his death in 1993. Today, granddaughter Lynsi looks over a chain of more than 300 stores.

The company has always considered itself a "family" for its long-standing practice of paying its employees more than the required minimum wage and offering benefits such as flexible scheduling and paid vacation time, generous perks by industry standards. As a result, the company has attracted motivated, friendly team members who reflect the burger stand's customer service philosophies.

While other fast food chains constantly look to innovate, the Snyder family business remains true to its roots: offering fresh, quality food at reasonable prices with outstanding customer service. And by not franchising their locations, they can ensure that customers receive consistently great food and service.

Who knows what the secret is to the Snyders' family success? Perhaps it is the secret sauce on their burgers – or the "secret menu" they offer regulars. Or maybe it's the inspiring Biblical scripture verses particularly observant patrons may notice on the bottom of their soda cups.

Or maybe it's that patrons can get "In-N-Out" quickly and affordably.

· · · · · · · · · ● · · · · · · · · · · ·

"A weakness of all human beings," Henry Ford said, "is trying to do too many things at once. That scatters effort and destroys direction. It makes for haste, and haste makes waste.

"Every now and then," Ford continued, "I wake up in the morning…with a dozen things I want to do. I know I can't do them all at once."

When asked what he did about that, Ford replied, "I go out and trot around the house. While I'm running off the excess energy that wants to do too much, my mind clears and I see what can be done and should be done first."

Are you focused? And, if so, what are you focused on? Remember, the acronym of FOCUS stands for "Follow One Course Until Success."

⋯⋯⋯⋯⋯⋅●⋅⋯⋯⋯⋯

The setting was the Olympic Games in Mexico City in 1968. The marathon was the final event on the program. The Olympic stadium was packed, and there was tremendous excitement as the first athlete, an Ethiopian runner, entered the stadium. The crowd erupted as he crossed the finish line.

Way back in the field was another runner, John Stephen Akwhari of Tanzania.

Approximately 12 miles into the 26.2-mile race, there was jostling between some runners, and Akwhari fell badly. He wounded his knee, and his shoulder also hit the pavement hard against the pavement. In fact, his leg was bleeding and his knee was apparently dislocated.

Medical staff urged him to withdraw.

However, Akhwari continued running. Actually, it was a mix of walking and a slow, limping run at points. There were 75 competitors at the start of the race that day, and 18 pulled out. All remaining runners eclipsed Akhwari, but the Tanzanian hobbled his way along the course, determined to finish.

An hour after the winner finished, Akwhari entered the stadium.

All but a few thousand of the crowd had gone home. John Stephen Akwhari moved around the track at a painstakingly slow pace, until finally he collapsed over the finish line to the cheers of those remaining.

It is one of the most heroic efforts of Olympic history. I actually get choked up about it as I write about it now.

Afterward, asked by a reporter why he had not dropped out, Akwhari said, "My country did not send me 10,000 miles just to start the race. They sent me to finish the race."

Wherever you are at today – if you've wandered or got distracted, if you've fallen and are hurting badly – whether it's your own fault or others have knocked you around – let John Stephen Akhwari encourage you: finish the race! Walking or running, stumbling or limping, it doesn't matter. Finish strong!

CHAPTER THIRTY-THREE

ju·bi·la·tion

/ˌjo͞obəˈlāSH(ə)n/

noun
1. a feeling of great happiness and triumph.

> "*True terror is to wake up one morning and discover that your high school class is running the country.*"
> — Kurt Vonnegut

Leaders laugh at themselves.

Life is too short, and I learned long ago that "I ain't all that – and neither are you!" Those who take themselves too seriously wind up looking like fools. If you think you know everything, I encourage you to teach kindergarten for one week. Those kids will set you straight.

I once had a little girl, Latisha, who raised her hand and asked, "Mr. Bercell (my students always pronounced my name that way), when are you gonna trim your nose hairs?"

"This afternoon," I replied, as I self-consciously covered my nose with my hand.

See – I'm not all that.

I have always considered myself first and foremost to be "a teacher." But that's really not accurate.

The longer I teach, the more I realize how little I know. And while I enjoy teaching all ages, my passion has always been with "the little ones" in preschool and early elementary school because they don't know what they don't know. That's a great lesson for all leaders.

Kids have a wonderful way of looking at the world because everything is new to them. They haven't been "trained yet," and my hope is that some of them manage to escape all their schooling without ever being inhibited by that training. They see the world in such refreshingly different ways than adults.

One of my favorite grades to teach was second grade. My seven- and eight-year-old students had so much energy and joy – sometimes, a bit too much.

One day, the kids wouldn't leave me alone. It was a constant stream of "Mr. Bercell?"

"Mr. Bercell?"

"Mr. Bercell?"

It was enough to drive me nuts!

Exasperated, I finally announced to my students, "Do you think you all could go just five minutes without someone saying 'Mr. Bercell.'"

The classroom got quiet, as my little ones shuffled in their seats – a bit baffled.

Then, little Laura raised her hand and hesitantly asked in her soft, sweet voice, "Um, Danny?"

· · · · · · · · · ● · · · · · · · · · ·

As much as I fondly remember my students, I grow to relish my former colleagues more and more as the years go by.

One of the first schools I taught at was located in the heart of "the hood" – an under-resourced community in South Central Los Angeles – and most of my colleagues were elderly African-American women from the South who had all been teaching for at least 20 years. Most were no-nonsense and a bit intimidating.

Mrs. Turner taught in the classroom beside me. She had been teaching for 40 years. She believed in two things: discipline and the Bible. The only way to get her to smile was to turn yourself upside down and look at her frown from the opposite angle.

You could not pair two more opposite human beings than Mrs. Turner and me.

But Mrs. Turner was my guardian angel who shielded me from our inept principal at the time. I adored Mrs. Turner. She helped me get through those first years, when I witnessed students who came from deplorable home environments. Her counsel saved me.

She also made me laugh.

Whenever she saw I had had a rough day, she'd share an anecdote from her years in the classroom. One, in particular, stood out.

Once she told her class of second graders to ask their parents for a family story with a moral at the end of it and to return the next day to tell their stories.

In class the next day, Marco gave his example first.

"My Papí is a farmer in Mexico, and we have chickens," Marco said. "One day we were taking lots of eggs to market in a basket on the front seat of the truck when we hit a big bump in the road. The basket fell off the seat and all the eggs broke.

"The moral of the story is not to put all your eggs in one basket."

"Very good," said Mrs. Turner.

Next, María raised her hand.

"My family raises chickens in our backyard," she said. "We had twenty eggs waiting to hatch, but when they did we only got ten chicks.

"The moral of the story is not to count your chickens before they're hatched."

"Very good," said Mrs. Turner, quite pleased with her students' responses.

Next, Richard Thomas raised his hand.

Mrs. Turner hesitated on calling on Richard Thomas, as he came from a broken home. His parents had abused him, so he was being raised by his grandparents. And Mrs. Turner knew his grandfather could often be "colorful" in his language and anecdotes.

Reluctantly, though, Mrs. Turner called on little Richard Thomas.

"My granddad told me this story about my grandma," Richard Thomas began. "Grandma was a flight engineer in World War II, and her plane got hit. She had to bail out over enemy territory, and all she had was a bottle of whiskey, a machine gun and a machete."

Intrigued by his story, all of the class – including Mrs. Turner – stared at Richard Thomas and waited to hear what happened next.

"Go on," Mrs. Turner insisted, and Richard Thomas happily obliged.

"Grandma drank all the whiskey as her plane went down," Richard Thomas continued. "Then she landed right in the middle of a hundred enemy soldiers. She killed seventy of them with the machine gun until she ran out of bullets.

"Then she killed twenty more with the machete 'til the blade broke.

"And then she killed the last ten with her bare hands!"

Almost everyone in the classroom stared at Richard Thomas with their mouths wide open in shock.

"Goodness gracious, Lord, have mercy," Mrs. Turner finally said. "What did your grandfather say was the moral of that frightening story?"

Richard Thomas grinned.

"Stay away from Grandma when she's been drinking."

I simply cannot fathom how people get through tough situations without laughing.

I have worked with great educational administrators and horrendous ones. And it soon became apparent that whenever I had a great administrator, I should praise God every day.

Mrs. Washington was one such administrator.

She knew when people needed a kick in the backside and when they needed a pat on the shoulder.

Faculty meetings had always been torturous to me, as I'm the sort of person who prefers to take action rather than form a committee to discuss it. But Mrs. Washington had such a kind way about her that my colleagues and I always participated and paid attention.

And Mrs. Washington, too, had a way of getting us all to laugh.

One day, after hearing a bunch of negative announcements – courtesy of our state's Department of Education – Mrs. Washington decided to share with us a positive note. Our school had recently held a luncheon in appreciation of the senior citizens from the nursing home down the street. They would come once a week to read to various classrooms at our school, and one woman, Mrs. Jackson – who, quite frankly, had a pretty ornery disposition – wanted to thank us for the radio she had won at the luncheon.

Mrs. Washington read aloud the elderly woman's letter word for word:

Dear Teachers and Staff:

God bless you all for the beautiful radio I won at your recent Senior Citizens luncheon.

I am 87 years old and have lived at (the nursing facility) for the past ten years. All of my family has passed away or forgotten about me. I am all alone, and it's nice to know that someone is thinking of me.

Mrs. Bradley has been my roommate for all my ten years here. She is 95 and has always had her own radio. But before I received one, she would never let me listen to hers, even when she was napping.

The other day, Mrs. Bradley's radio fell off her nightstand and broke into a million pieces. It was awful, and she was in tears. Her distress over the broken radio touched me, and I knew this was God's way of answering my prayers.

She asked if she could listen to my new radio, and I told her to kiss my backside.

Thank you for that opportunity.

Sincerely,
Yolanda Jackson

* * * * * * * * * ● * * * * * * * * * *

It wasn't easy teaching in the inner city.

Some of my students experienced horrors that I cannot or, rather, choose not to imagine. In fact, many of their stories made me cry myself to sleep on many nights.

But what got me through those tough times were funny and uplifting tales – stories. They came from my students, my colleagues – lots of places. I kept a journal inside my desk, and I would write down those anecdotes.

And whenever I had one of those days that I wanted to forget, I would re-read those stories, to keep my spirits up.

It's not easy being a leader, but all of us are leaders. At a very minimum, we each lead ourselves.

Leadership begins with motivation. But it is so much more.

I hope you use this book to guide you, remembering that *you are the one*.

You are the one that can make others scowl...or smile.

You are the one that has the power to discourage... or encourage.

You...are the one.

AFTERWORD

Some people collect stamps, while others amass baseball cards.

I've always collected stories.

Ever since I was little, sitting on the lap of my Grandpa (a grand ole Irishman from New York), I have been fascinated with anecdotes. Listening to Paul Harvey on the radio, I have had a life-long obsession with spinning a good yarn.

When my editor asked me to create a bibliography for this book, I didn't know where to begin. Sure, I could Google each story and try to find the exact source. But that isn't the point of this book.

I wrote this book to lift you up. Good tales have always been my sanctuary. I wanted to share some of my favorites with you, in hopes they would lift you up.

Are the stories in this book original to me?

Some are. Most aren't.

You may have heard some of them before. That wouldn't surprise me.

But if you managed to get through this book without learning anything new, I'd chalk that up to ignorance (uh-oh, I just offended three of you).

Speaking to tens of thousands of people, I have learned that there are some people who will never be satisfied. You can give them 83 ideas, and they'll complain you didn't give them 96.

You can describe a beautiful Spring day outside, and they'll moan about how dirty the window is that you're looking through.

These people choose to be offended. They used to suck the energy out from me like Dementors in the *Harry Potter* books. And then I realized it's not worth worrying about a few curmudgeons when most people get a kick out of my collection. To each, his own.

If you didn't enjoy the book, here's an idea: give the book to someone else. And find yourself another book. There are over 300,000 printed every year, and I am sure you can find one that is just right for you.

Life's short. My final piece of wisdom is this: leaders can't please everybody. And those who try, as a wise person once said, are sure to please none!

Regardless, I sincerely wish you the best of success in *your* journey. God bless you.

Suggested Readings

"Not all readers are leaders," President Harry S. Truman said. "But all leaders are readers." While there are present-day exceptions to that rule, I would suggest that all effective leaders are avid readers. They are constantly curious.

While I may have short-changed you on a bibliography, I did want to include a list of some books on my shelves that I have turned to for guidance and inspiration:

Education/Teaching

Braithwaite, E.R. (1967). *To sir, with love.* New York: Pyramid Books.

Codell, E. R. (2001). *Educating Esmé: Diary of a teacher's first year.* Chapel Hill, NC: Algonquin Books.

Collins, M., & Tamarkin, C. (1990). *Marva Collins' way.* New York: Jeremy P. Tarcher/Putnam.

Conroy, P. (1972). *The water is wide*. New York: Houghton Mifflin.

Cullinan, B.E. (1992). *Read to me: Raising kids who love to read*. New York: Scholastic.

Dryden, G., & Vos, J. (1999). *The learning revolution*. Torrance, CA: The Learning Web.

Esquith, R. (2007). *Teach like your hair's on fire: The methods and madness inside Room 56*. New York: Viking.

Feynman, R.P. (1985). *Surely you're joking, Mr. Feynman: Adventures of a curious character*. New York: W.W. Norton & Co.

Fox, M. (2001). *Reading magic: Why reading aloud to our children will change their lives forever*. San Diego, CA: Harvest Original.

Fulghum, R. (1988). *All I really need to know I learned in kindergarten*. New York: Villard Books.

Johnson, L. (1994). *My posse don't do homework*. New York: St. Martin's Press.

Kohl, H. (1967). *36 children*. New York: Plume.

Kotlowitz, A. (1991). *There are no children here: The story of two boys growing up in the other America*. New York: Nan A. Talese/Doubleday.

Kozol, J. (1991). *Savage inequalities*. New York: Crown Publishers.

Krashen, S. (1993). *The power of reading*. Englewood, CO: Libraries Unlimited, Inc.

McCourt, F. (2005). *Teacher man: A memoir.* New York: Scribner.

Miller, D. (2009). *The book whisperer.* San Francisco: Jossey-Bass

Ryan Madson, P. (2005). *Improv wisdom: Don't prepare, just show up.* New York: Bell Tower.

Swope, S. (2005). *I am a pencil: A teacher, his kids, and their world of stories.* New York: Owl Books.

Trelease, J. (2006). *The read-aloud handbook* (6th ed.). New York: Penguin Books.

Psychology/Business

Ariely, D. (2008). *Predictably irrational: The hidden forces that shape our decisions.* New York: HarperCollins.

Brafman, O., & Brafman, R. (2008). *Sway: The irresistible pull of traditional behavior.* New York: Broadway Books.

Brafman, O., & Brafman, R. (2010). *Click: The forces behind how we fully engage with people, work, and everything we do.* New York: Crown Business.

Carnegie, D. (1990). *How to win friends and influence people (reissue).* New York: Pocket Books.

Chabris, C., & Simons, D. (2009). *The invisible gorilla: And other ways our intuitions deceive us.* New York: Broadway Paperbacks.

Cialdini, R. (1984). *Influence: The psychology of persuasion.* New York: HarperCollins.

Cialdini, R. (2016). *Pre-suasion: A revolutionary way to influence and persuade.* New York: Simon & Schuster.

Colvin, G. (2008). *Talent is overrated: What really separates world-class performers from everybody else.* New York: Portfolio.

Cowen, T. (2007). *Discover your inner economist: Use incentives to fall in love, survive your next meeting, and motivate your dentist.* New York: Plume.

Coyle, D. (2009). *The talent code: Greatness isn't born. It's grown. Here's how.* New York: Bantam Books.

Csikszentmihalyi, M. (1990). *Flow: The psychology of optimal experience.* New York: HarperPerennial.

De Bono, E. (1985). *Six thinking hats.* New York: Back Bay Books.

Duhigg, C. (2012). *The power of habit: Why we do what we do in life and business*. New York: Random House.

Dweck, C. (2006). *Mindset: The new psychology of success.* New York: Ballantine Books.

Gladwell, M. (2000). *The tipping point: How little things can make a big difference.* New York: Back Bay Books.

Gladwell, M. (2005). *Blink: The power of thinking without thinking.* New York: Back Bay Books.

Gladwell, M. (2008). *Outliers: The story of success.* New York: Back Bay Books.

Grant, A. (2013). *Give and take: The hidden social dynamics of success.* New York: Penguin Books.

Heath, C., & Heath, D. (2007). *Made to stick: Why some ideas survive and others die.* New York: Random House.

Heath, C., & Heath, D. (2010). *Switch: How to change things when change is hard.* New York: Crown Publishing.

Hogan, K. (1996). *The psychology of persuasion: How to persuade others to your way of thinking.* Gretna, LA: Pelican Publishing.

Lemov, D., Woolway, E., & Yezzi, K. (2012). *Practice perfect: 42 rules for getting better at getting better.* San Francisco: Jossey Bass.

Levitt, S.D., & Dubner, S.J. (2009). *Freakanomics: A rogue economist explores the hidden side of everything.* New York: William Morrow.

Peale, N.V. (1952). *The power of positive thinking.* New York: Fawcett Crest.

Pink, D. (2005). *A whole new mind: Moving from the Information Age to the Conceptual Age.* New York: Riverhead Books.

Pink, D. (2009). *Drive: The surprising truth about what motivates us.* New York: Riverhead Books.

Pressfield, S. (2002). *The war of art: Winning the inner creative battle.* New York: Warner Books.

Seligman, M. (2002). *Authentic happiness: Using the new positive psychology to realize your potential for lasting fulfillment.* New York: Free Press.

Simmons, G. (2014). *Me, Inc.: Build an army of one, unleash your inner rock God, win in life and business.* New York: HarperCollins.

Stevenson, M. (2011). *Becoming a hypnotic influence ninja.* Tustin, CA: Transform Destiny.

Thaler, R.H., & Sunstein, C.R. (2008). *Nudge: Improving decisions about health, wealth, and happiness.* New York: Penguin Books.

Wansink, B. (2006). Mindless eating: Why we eat more than we think. New York: Bantam Books.

Success/Leadership/Personal Development

Ash, M.K. (1981). *Miracles happen.* New York: HarperCollins.

Aurandt, P. (1980). *More of Paul Harvey's The Rest of the Story.* New York: Bantam Books.

Aurandt, P. (1983). *Destiny and 102 other real life mysteries.* New York: Bantam Books.

Blair, G.R. (2010). *Everything counts: 52 remarkable ways to inspire excellence and drive results.* Hoboken, NJ: John Wiley & Sons.

Blanchard, K., & Johnson, S. (1981). *The one minute manager.* New York: William Morrow & Company.

Blanchard, K., Lacinak, T., Tompkins, C., & Ballard, J. (2002). *Whale done! The power of positive relationships.* New York: Free Press.

Boyle, G. (2010). *Tattoos on the heart: The power of boundless compassion.* New York: Free Press.

Canfield, J. (2005). *The success principles: How to get from where you are to where you want to be.* New York: HarperCollins.

Clear, J. (2018). *Atomic habits: An easy and proven way to build good habits & break bad ones*. New York: Avery.

Corcoran, B. (2003). *If you don't have big breasts, put ribbons on your pigtails & other lessons I learned from my mom.* New York: Portfolio.

Covey, S. (1989). *The seven habits of highly effective people: Restoring the character ethic.* New York: Fireside.

Croce, P. (2000). *I feel great and you will too! An inspiring journey of success with practical tips on how to score big in life.* Philadelphia: Running Press.

Diamandis, P. (2012). *Abundance: The future is better than you think.* New York: Free Press.

Dyer, W. (2006). *Inspiration: Your ultimate calling.* Carlsbad, CA: Hay House.

Elrod, H. (2012). *The miracle morning: The not-so-obvious secret guaranteed to transform your life before 8 am.* Los Angeles: Hal Elrod.

Farber, S. (2009). *The radical edge: Stoke your business, amp your life, and change the world.* New York: Kaplan Publishing.

Ferriss, T. (2007). *The 4-hour workweek: Escape 9-5, live anywhere, and join the new rich.* New York: Crown Publishing.

Frankl, V. (1959). *Man's search for meaning.* New York: Washington Square Press.

Freiberg, K., & Freiberg, J. (1996). *Nuts! Southwest Airlines' crazy recipe for business and personal success.* New York: Bard Press.

Gawande, A. (2010). *The checklist manifesto: How to get things right.* New York: Picador.

Griffith, S. (2019). *The time cleanse: A proven system to eliminate wasted time, realize your full potential, and reinvest in what matters most.* New York: McGraw Hill Education.

Hardy, D. (2010). *The compound effect: Multiplying your success. One simple step at a time.* Lake Dallas, TX: Success Books.

Hill, N. (1960). *Think and grow rich.* New York: Fawcett.

Holtz, L. (1998). *Winning every day.* New York: Collins.

Lundin, S.C., Paul, H., & Christensen, J. (2000). *Fish: A proven way to boost morale and improve results.* New York: Hyperion.

Mackay, H. (1988). *Swim with the sharks without being eaten alive: Outsell, outmanage, outmotivate, and outnegotiate your competition.* New York: Ivy Books.

Maltz, M. (1960). *Psycho-cybernetics.* New York: Pocket Books.

Mandino, O. (1968). *The greatest salesman in the world.* New York: Bantam Books.

Maxwell, J. (1993). *Developing the leader within you.* Nashville, TN: Thomas Nelson.

Maxwell, J. (1998). *The 21 irrefutable laws of leadership.* Nashville, TN: Thomas Nelson.

Maxwell, J. (2001). *The 17 indisputable laws of teamwork.* Nashville, TN: Thomas Nelson.

McKeown, G. (2014). *Essentialism: the disciplined pursuit of less.* New York: Crown Business.

Osteen, J. 2004). *Your best life now: 7 steps to living at your full potential.* New York: Warner Faith.

Peale, N.V. (1952). *The power of positive thinking.* New York: Fawcett Crest.

Posada, J.D., & Singer, E. (2005). *Don't eat the marshmallow – yet! The secret to sweet success in work and life.* New York: Berkley Publishing.

Riley, P. (1994). *The winner within: A life plan for team players.* New York: Berkley.

Robbins, A. (1997). *Unlimited power: The new science of personal achievement (reprint).* New York: Fireside.

Robinson, K. (2009). *The element: How finding your passion changes everything.* New York: Penguin.

Rohn, E.J. (1981). *The seasons of life.* Southlake, TX: Jim Rohn International.

Rowe, M. (2019). *The way I heard it.* New York: Gallery Books.

Schwartz, D.J. (1959). *The magic of thinking big.* New York: Fireside.

Shallenberger, S. (2015). *Becoming your best: The 12 principles of highly successful leaders.* New York: McGraw Hill Education.

Sharma, R. (1997). *The monk who sold his Ferrari: A fable about fulfilling your dreams and reaching your destiny.* New York: HarperOne.

Sinek, S. (2009). *Start with why: How great leaders inspire everyone to take action.* New York: Portfolio.

Syed, M. (2010). *Bounce: Mozart, Federer, Picasso, Beckham, and the science of success.* New York: HarperCollins.

Tracy, B. (1993). *Maximum achievement: Strategies and skills that will unlock your hidden powers to succeed.* New York: Fireside.

Von Oech, R. (1998). *A whack on the side of the head* (3rd ed.). New York: Warner Books.

Vujicic, N. (2012). *Unstoppable: The incredible power of faith in action.* Colorado Springs, CO: Waterbrook Press.

Waitley, D. (1983) *Seeds of greatness: The ten best-kept secrets of total success.* Old Tappan, NJ: Fleming H. Revell Company.

Warren, R. (2002). *The purpose-driven life: What on Earth am I here for?* Grand Rapids, MI: Zondervan.

Williamson, P.B. (1982). *Patton's principles.* New York: Touchstone.

Wooden, J. (2003). *They call me coach.* New York: McGraw-Hill.

Zander, R.S., & Zander, B. (2002). *The art of possibility.* New York: Penguin.

Ziglar, Z. (1997). *Over the top.* Nashville, TN: Thomas Nelson.

Acknowledgments

I have been blessed to work with wonderful people around the globe – leaders in education, industry, athletics and government – and I have been mentored by a wide array of wonderful people.

The authors and thought leaders who have had a tremendous impact on me include Edmund Morris, David McCullough, Jon Meacham, Doris Kearns Goodwin, Zig Ziglar, Og Mandino, Rick Warren, Joel Osteen, William Manchester, Lin Manuel Miranda, Ron Chernow, Walter Isaacson, Jack Canfield, John Maxwell, Michael Port, Michael Hyatt, Donald Miller, Jim Rohn, Tony Robbins, Dean Graziosi, Alfie Kohn, Rafe Esquith, Sir Ken Robinson, John Feinstein, Bryant Gumbel, Bob Costas, Vin Scully, Richard Feynman, Bill Simmons and Mike Rowe. I have never met any of you, but know you have all influenced me greatly.

Personal friends and mentors include Matt Schaefer (my oldest and dearest friend), Andrew Lyons, Rob Schwartz, Adam LeVrier, Jordan Henry, Joe Martin,

Rob Lloyd-Still, Steven Griffith, Donna Whyte, Melissa Dickson, Steve & Lynne Ecenbarger, Hal Elrod, Ruben Gonzalez, Pat Quinn, Pete Vargas, Rob Shallenberger, Steve Shallenberger, Jimmy Nelson, Jamie Thorup, Peter Bohlinger, Ryan Anderson, Travis Boyd, Jeff Arnott, Sharon Russell, Kirk Kirkwood, Ernest Black, Andre & Barbara Garner, Jeff Dousharm, Brod Bagert, Bruce Lansky, Nile Stanley, Rick Davis, Russell Verhey, Gary Barnes, Roger Nielsen, Andrea Adams-Miller, Scott Stratten, Jim & Lilli Grant, Wilene Dunn, Jamie Cohen, Jeff & Cynthia Snyder, Jonathan Sprinkles, Michael & Kayla Stevenson, Sara McDaniel, Debbie Silver, Scott Keffer, Kurt Black, Ryan Giffen, Jeff Flamm, Karen & Gordy Brown, Tim Clue, Todd Loewenstein, Angela Ray, Julie Reardon, Dona Rippley, the Haradons (Mike, Penni, Hollie & Dave), Taquan Stewart, Val Brown & John Manders, Dennis Yu, Brad Lea, Shane Therault, Sandra Haseley, David Waldy, Harry Petsanis, Jerome & Tracey Carter, Clarissa Duskin, Lori Ozckus, Virginia Barkley, Ron Seaver, Eric & Leslie Mueller, Eric Trules, Steven Fischer, Greg & B.J. O'Donnell, David Yaden, Sam Belmonte, Mike & Betty Carroll, Bong Miquiabas, David & Kari Bilik, LaVonna Roth, Travis Brown, Mike Wolf, Alex Kajitani, Dave Burgess, Kathy Perez, Kim Burke, Mike Dalton, Jason Bittner, Dave Navarro, Kevin & Linda Buck, Miah Callihan, Dan Parkins, Richard Cash, Katie McKnight, Robin Keefe, DeVere Wolsey, Petra Griffin, Diane Lapp, Doug Fisher, Stacey Thomas, Nancy Frey, Tim Rasinski, Mike

McQueen, Rob & Tracy Cota, Bart Christianson, Dave Espino, Jim Johnson, Kevin Clayson, Mark Eaton, Jim Warner, Kevin Knight, Angela Coombs, Scotty Ramos, Rachelle Cracchiolo, Archie Pazos, Evan Robb, Laura Robb, Alan Sitomer, Cat Crews, Sue Crum, Ruth Culham, the Daddonas (Steve, Vincent & Steven), Wayne & Janae Dahl, Marti Day Folck, Jerry Wooden, Janice Gerson, Lee Gardenswartz, Anita Rowe, Michelle Prince, Katie Decker, Jim Trelease, Stephen Krashen, Kurt & Laurie Driskill, Edgar Vann, Kevin Eastman, Bill Packard, Jana Echevarria, Mary Ellen Vogt, Jake Kelfer, Jerry Edwards, Kevin & Wendy Forman, Chris Cannon, Mike & LeAnn Fritz, Beth Fung, Marc Fulson, Kristin Shreve, Corinne Burton, Lisa Ketchum, Donalyn Miller, Brett Pate, Doug Towne, Deanne Mendoza, Andrew Garratt, Sourena Vasseghi, Fernando Perez, Dave Jesiolowski, Jaymin Patel, Sherry Winn, Trish Garza, Forest Hamilton, Kim Graves, Fernando Marquez, Gary Schill, Kalani Vale, Davy Tyburski, Matt Jones, Ben Keel, Wayne Logue, Dan Dedekian, K. Nehru, Hide & Yumiko Kojima, Ted Prodromou, Barry & Barbara Wishner, Hal Urban, Greg Tang, Eric LeMoine, Kate Maggs, Bob Matulich, Andy Miller, Chris Miller, Jeff Miller, Dorothy Paige, David Dodson, Gautam Rao, Gloria Rodriguez, Kurt Schwengel, Harold & Lynden Smith, Karen Mohr, Bob Sornson, Mike Tomasello, Jeff Veley, Chris Warner, Jay Tan, Suzanne Witmer, Chase Young, Frank Buck and Andy Hargreaves. Thank you all for being part of my life.

I would also like to thank the tens of thousands of students and seminar attendees I have worked with over the years throughout North America, Asia, Europe and Africa. Looking forward to continuing my work in all those places and expanding to South America, Australia and Antarctica in the future!

I have been blessed to get to share a business with my friend, Nestor Santtia. He is a man of action who constantly inspires me to achieve more.

While I dedicated this book to my incredible parents, I have also been blessed with an amazing brother and sister. Jim and Liz – thank you.

Finally, I am grateful to my wife, Jeanie, and my three children – Kate, Sean and Samantha. Thank you all for giving me a reason to be better every day.

CONNECT WITH DANNY ON SOCIAL MEDIA

 ReadBETTERin67Steps.com
The World's Leading Reading
Engagement Program

 DannyBrassell.com

 Danny@DannyBrassell.com

 YouTube.com/DannyBrassell

 @DannyBrassell #DannySpeaks

FaceBook.com/DannyBrassell

 LinkedIn.com/in/DannyBrassell

instagram.com/realdannybrassell

Make sure to get your free bonus gifts, including an e-copy of Danny's book *Read, Lead & Succeed: 50 Simple Ways to Produce Extraordinary Results in Business and Life* and digital versions of his popular live trainings for parents and teachers, *My 5 Biggest Secrets to Getting Your Kid to Love Reading* and *8 Big Ideas to Help Your Child Become a Better Reader.*

Simply go to:
www.FreeGiftfromDanny.com

Interested in becoming a better reader, but you don't think you can find the time to read? Then you should join www.lazyreaders.com, where we provide short books for busy people. Every month you will receive 10 book recommendations: 3-4 adult-level, 3-4 young adult-level and 3-4 children's books all under 250 pages. Your subscription is FREE.

We Transform Struggling and Reluctant Readers into More Passionate and Proficient Readers.

If Your Child Struggles to Read or Dislikes Reading, It Is Imperative That You **Take Action Now** to Change That.

INTERACTIVE VIDEO MODULES

Introducing: Quick Tips at Your Fingertips. You've seen plenty of long, thick parenting and education books; but why not watch an expert teach you specific strategies instantly? Available on any device.

AUDIO LESSONS AND NUGGETS

Listen to INSANELY POWERFUL audio lessons and inspiring motivational nuggets that will inspire you and your child and give you massive jolts of ideas, creativity, motivation and learning. Whether on your commute, listening from home or at the gym: we've got you covered.

ACTION GUIDE & CHEAT SHEETS

Review every strategy in ten minutes or less, using our proprietary action guide, filled with daily reflection activities. Convenient for quickly finding your favorite strategies.

MEMBER DISCUSSIONS

Social learning is key. Network with like minded, powerful individuals and participate in LIVE sessions with other parents and educators JUST LIKE YOU! This is the most effective Mastermind you'll ever be a part of; and it's included for FREE with your membership.

Join Now!
and Claim Your FREE Bonuses

Help Your Child Read MORE, Read BETTER and LOVE Reading. Take the Next Step, and Help Your Child Become a Reader for Life!

Go to: www.ReadBETTERin67Steps.com

The World's Leading Reading Engagement System

Affectionately known as "Jim Carrey with a Ph.D." and "America's Leading Reading Ambassador," Dr. Danny Brassell has held a variety of titles and worked with leaders from a variety of fields and disciplines, but he has always considered himself first and foremost a teacher. He is a top-selling author of 15 books, including *The Reading Breakthrough* and *The Reading Makeover*, based on his popular TEDx talk. For the past 25 years he has also been a lecturer and professor at a number of universities, including his current position as a faculty advisor for the CalStateTEACH program and distinguished visiting professor at the American University of Cairo. A gregarious, sought-after author, speaker, accountability coach and business consultant, Danny is a recognized authority on leadership development, reading, motivation and communication skills and the co-founder of www. ReadBETTERin67steps.com, the world's top reading engagement program. His mission is to bring joy back into education and the workplace. Thousands, from school districts to businesses to association conferences, have enjoyed his energetic, interactive and informative presentations. He has spoken to over 3,000 different audiences worldwide.